Fairy Gardening

Fairy Gardening

Creating Your Own Magical Miniature Garden

Julie Bawden-Davis *and* Beverly Turner

Photography by Xuong Do, Happy Photos

Skyhorse Publishing

Skyhorse Publishing books may be purchased in bulk at special discounts for sales promotion, corporate gifts, fund-raising, or educational purposes. Special editions can also be created to specifications. For details, contact the Special Sales Department, Skyhorse Publishing, 307 West 36th Street, 11th Floor, New York, NY 10018 or info@skyhorsepublishing.com.

Skyhorse® and Skyhorse Publishing® are registered trademarks of Skyhorse Publishing, Inc.®, a Delaware corporation.

Visit our website at www.skyhorsepublishing.com.

10 9 8 7 6 5 4 3 2 1

Library of Congress Cataloging-in-Publication Data is available on file.

ISBN: 978-1-61608-833-0

Bawden-Davis, Julie.
  Fairy gardening : creating your own magical miniature garden / Julie Bawden-Davis and Beverly Turner; photography by Xuong Do.
      p. cm.
  ISBN 978-1-61608-833-0 (pbk. : alk. paper)
  1. Gardens, Miniature. 2. Miniature plants. 3. Gardens, Miniature—Pictorial works. 4. Miniature plants—Pictorial works. I. Turner, Beverly. II. Title.
  SB433.5.B375 2013
  635—dc23
                              2012038234

Printed in China

For Allan, whose love and support are everything. For sister Sue, brother Bruce, and Mom, who taught us how to be happy.

—B. T.

CONTENTS

Foreword

Maybe I never outgrew my Barbies. Or maybe, as my mom laughingly once said, "You've always just loved miniatures! Remember the fort you made out of sugar cubes for extra credit in third grade?" I do. The project was inspired by a yellow plastic cannon I found in a box of Cracker Jacks.

I still love miniatures. So much so that some years ago I decided that even though I was an adult, I wanted to build the dollhouse of my dreams. At the hobby store, I found a basic model and proceeded to do a little kit-bashing. In other words, I took that classic Edwardian-style dollhouse included in the kit and added on to it. And added. And added. And added. By the time I finished, my diminutive home had a garden rivaling Central Park! It was huge! The dollhouse and its sprawling garden became the center of attention when company came to visit.

After several years of friends asking, "Don't you wish you could have a real garden that's as tiny as this?" I thought, why not? As head designer at M & M Nursery in Orange, California, I started experimenting with different plants to see how easily they adapted to a small-scale look. In the beginning, herbs and a few bonsai-type "trees" were the only plants available. Fast-forward twelve years and there are several hundred dwarf plant varieties suitable to different climates and zones. Some major garden suppliers now manufacture accessories specifically for fairy landscaping, and the staggering number of people discovering this delightful hobby climbs daily!

Watching people's faces when they first encounter fairy gardens is a little like seeing kids finding everything they want under the tree on Christmas morning. Astonishment gives way to pure pleasure as people inspect every inch of these enchanting mini landscapes. Somehow, fairy gardens transport us to a place far from the mundane tasks of everyday life and into a realm of wonder and imagination. Fairy gardens remind us that we are never too old to play "Let's pretend."

One of the best aspects of fairy gardening for me is watching people share their enthusiasm with each other. Mothers and daughters come to the nursery to work on their creations, as do couples, siblings, and even entire families, who plan a fairy project with everyone having a hand in it. Obviously, I'm not the only one with a fondness for miniatures!

Since that first fairy garden, my designs have become more sophisticated over the years. At fairy gardening how-to seminars, I answered questions and mentally tucked them away to share at the next lecture. I thought I had just about every detail covered until I had an "aha" moment at the Southern California Spring Garden Show in 2009. Every year at this popular event, local nurseries and landscapers showcase their best plants, garden supplies, and horticultural ideas. For many seasons, we brought examples of my fairy gardens, but this time another nursery had them as well. Curious, I enlisted my sister's help to indulge in a little friendly "fairy espionage."

Sue is the best big sister anyone could ask for and a great first grade teacher. In fact, from what I can see, her only flaw is that she didn't inherit the family love of gardening! But this comes in handy when I drag her to events like the garden show, because I get to "see" things through her fresh eyes. So I pulled a hat low on my brow and wore my biggest Jackie O sunglasses to snoop my way over to the display. After a quick peek, I scuttled off in the opposite direction. A few minutes later, Sue joined me.

"So?" I asked.

"Of course I'm prejudiced because you're my sister," she said. "But those other fairy gardens just didn't work for me. They looked like a pot full of plants with a fairy stuck in it. Yours look like real, live, mini gardens. Why is that?"

I replied that I simply take the time to choose just the right plants and accessories.

"But the main thing is, with every fairy garden I make, I try to tell a little story," I said. "That's what makes the difference. I want it to seem as if a teeny somebody actually lives there."

This book is the culmination of more than a decade of designing fairy gardens with those tiny inhabitants in mind.

In here you'll find my tips, tricks, and secrets, and, most importantly, you'll encounter the very best ways to create a garden filled with heart. Your heart. As you take the fairy gardening journey, let your imagination soar and have fun!

Beverly Turner
Head Designer
M & M Nursery, Orange, California
www.fairygardenexpert.net

Fairy Gardening

Chapter 1

Developing a Theme

Deciding on a theme is the best way to begin making plans for your fairy garden. Once you know the basic subject, designing your garden comes easily. Think of all the occasions in your life when you rely on a particular theme to give you direction. As a kid, how many times did you agonize over what to be for Halloween, yet as soon as you decided on a costume, such as a witch, you found it easy to choose the perfect make-up and accessories? How about birthday parties? Pirates or princesses? Sweet sixteen or over-the-hill? Once you decide on the theme, it all seems to fall naturally into place. No skull-and-crossbones flags for a princess party, but pink, sparkly wands and tiaras instead. Hosting a dozen "royal" girls determines the food, the décor, and the entertainment.

A theme helps you choose all of the necessary elements that, when combined, create a miniature world filled with little scenes that seem to come to life right before your eyes. Knowing the topic of your garden helps you choose just the right materials like focal piece, container, and accessories.

Victorian Charm

One of the most popular themes is a classic Victorian cutting garden. Instead of stopping at the market for a quick bouquet, Victorian-era ladies filled their yards with every flower they could imagine. And rather than selecting a few varieties and repeating them throughout the landscape, as is common now, they instead planted a charming mix of blooms all together. These floral borders sat cordoned off by fencing from lush expanses of lawn, and stepping stones and pea gravel pathways served as sidewalks. Potted plants, gazing balls, birdbaths, fountains, and cast-iron furniture decorated most of these gardens. And in order to shrink that turn-of-the-century atmosphere to one small container, a few such well-placed accessories give the suggestion of an artfully arranged, Victorian outdoor space.

Scaling down doesn't just mean using mini accessories—it also refers to the size and quantity of your plant material. Whereas a Victorian yard might have dozens of blooming perennials in the same bed, cramming that many into one pot will overwhelm your fairy scene. Just five or six miniature plants nestled behind a little fence in a 16-inch pot will create a botanical explosion, and a 6-inch-wide patch of moss will lend the impression of a large, rambling lawn. Likewise, four "trees" under-planted with varying shades of green groundcover suddenly resembles a thick forest.

Mini-tip: Understanding Scale

As we go through all the stages of what makes a successful fairy garden, keep in mind that we are working in the classic miniature scale of 1:12. This means that one inch in miniature equals one foot in real life. So a 4-inch fairy figurine is equivalent to a 4-foot child. An arbor at your home that towers 7 feet tall would only stand 7 inches high in the miniature world. Until you become accustomed to this scale, be sure to keep a tape measure handy as you scout around for goodies to add to your fairy garden.

Pint-size Royalty

Through the centuries, mankind's desire to control nature has resulted in some of the loveliest spots on earth. Many of the finest examples of landscape design originated in the courts of eighteenth-century France. Sumptuous knot gardens with elaborate scrollwork of tidy hedges were the result of meticulous work by the king's gardeners. The fact that these gardens were only intended for visual pleasure and provided no food elevated them to royal status. Only the wealthiest of men could afford such frivolous use of the land.

Most of these formal French gardens were meant to be viewed from an upper landing, where one could take in a long vista all at once. Curvy lines of plantings resembling lace when seen from above complemented borders of very straight rows of trees and bushes. Long stretches of pathways led to various garden rooms planted in grid-like precision. Statuary and urns of seasonal botanicals decorated the garden, often in repeated patterns for greater impact.

In replicating a formal garden for a smaller pot, keep in mind that straight lines are much easier to deal with and don't take up as much room as interlocking curves. A square-shaped container works well with this style and makes planning your royal retreat much simpler. Starting with a focal point prominently centered at the back, like an arch or architectural piece, fill in the surrounding area with plants on each side. Once done, you will have a solid row consisting of plants-arch-plants across the back of the pot. Divide the remaining space in front of this back row into four squares. Whatever you put in one section, repeat it in the other three. Linear pathways of tiny crushed rock or miniature bricks aid the crisp, formal look. Any intersection where two paths cross is just the place to showcase a teensy statue.

Mini-tip: Fashionable Formal Planters

Drill a hole (for drainage) in matching saucers, and plant groundcovers in them. This creates instant formal-edged flower beds that can be arranged in a variety of patterns.

Rustic Retreat

If a formal look isn't to your taste, a rustic garden might be just the thing. Gift shops featuring country décor and craftware are great spots for finding the more rugged essentials. Many such stores offer lighted houses in the style of a cabin. Remove the bulb and cord and you have an ideal mountain getaway. The back of the piece will have a hole where the light bulb was inserted. Cover the opening with a small "shrub" and keep the rest of the plantings surrounding the cabin simple. One tree and some low foliage, such as creeping thyme or baby's tears, are enough. A line of small, flat rocks leading from the edge of the pot to the front door creates a welcoming entrance, and a length of twig and wire fence may be all the accessories you need. Of course, an animal or two always lends a sense of whimsy and life to the scene.

Inspiration is all around you—literally in your own backyard. Do you or a friend love to dig in the dirt? If so, what tools do you use? If there's an area where you stow away old pots and watering cans, take a step back and study that composition. Think about copying what you see in front of you in your own miniature garden. The everyday, mundane terra-cotta and tools somehow completely captivate when in fairy size. Your potting bench might not be the first thing you want guests to see when they visit for a barbecue, but a miniature version of the same scene is sure to be the hit of the party.

Walk around your yard and look for the ordinary things that state "someone lives here." What about that pile of kid's toys under a tree? Even in Fairyland, children leave their playthings out! A dish of water near a doghouse or a hose no one bothered to coil up are both recognizable objects to which everyone can relate and such items will make your fairy garden come to life.

Out of the Ordinary

Don't limit yourself to a standard definition of "garden." Your theme can be a reflection of a place or area somewhere close to home or on the other side of the world. If you live in the mountains, why not try a desert scene? If your apartment building is a modern tower of steel and glass, place a little farm on your balcony just to make you smile. Remember, these containers are representations of real life, but you are the one who can decide what fun things to put in them! Fantasy and imagination are far more important than accuracy, so if you want a waterfall in the middle of the desert, go for it. After all, this might not be the actual Mojave, but rather the arid outskirts of a fairy forest!

Selecting appropriate plants makes upkeep of your fairyland easy. If you like the drought-tolerant appearance of a dry climate, plant small succulents, cacti, and sedums. Tossing a moisture-loving flowering shrub into such a landscape makes things difficult, as the plants have different watering requirements and one group will ultimately end up suffering. When looking for plants that fit your design, don't forget the 1:12 scale. Suddenly, the tiny berries on something like a cotoneaster become apples. Just two of these "trees" standing next to each other create the idea of an orchard of fruit ripe for the harvest.

Mini Memoryscapes

What could be better than using a favorite childhood memory to inspire your miniature garden? Every spring, the scent of roses and pine needles still brings to mind happy days as a six-year-old when I (Beverly) visited a beloved neighbor's yard. Magic happened as I stepped through an ivy-covered arch into a tiny grove

of three intertwined pines that created a secret cave. As an ambassador to the far-off land that only allowed children, a resident dog greeted me as I sprawled on the thick cushion created by years of dropped needles to read a book. With a fountain trickling in the background in that sacred space, I drifted away from the confines of suburban reality. Even now, as an adult, that feeling of secure serenity bubbles up at the recollection of that time. A secret garden in miniature captures the essence of that memory, bringing me a little joy on a daily basis.

Don't be afraid to choose a theme that seems a bit unconventional. Years ago at M & M Nursery, a young boy came in with his mom to look at the displays. After a few visits, he declared, "I really like these, but I'm a guy. I don't want to make one with a fairy." After being assured that he could create any kind of miniature garden he wanted, Tyler decided that a space-age moon garden would be a great theme for him. The result was an imaginative lunarscape filled with succulents of all shapes and accented with rocks gathered during family vacations. Plastic robots completed the scene, which had a decidedly masculine flair. The garden was wonderful and a true reflection of the fantastic little boy who made it.

So let your theme flaunt your interests. Show your love of horses by creating a meadow inhabited by a grazing equine figurine, or allow your inner surfer to take refuge in a planting edged with sand and overlooking an "ocean" of blue glass. Anything you love can be translated into a miniature setting.

Telling Tales

Perhaps a cherished book or childhood story begs to be brought to life. Think of your garden as a three-dimensional illustration of a favorite chapter or as a representation of the overall feel of the story. *Alice in Wonderland* is a good example of a beloved classic that translates well to a miniature garden. Although the wonderland book is separate from *Through the Looking Glass* (which was a sequel penned six years later), the characters have been meshed together in so many of the filmed versions that they all seem to live in the same place. Ultimately, it isn't important knowing which book they came from, only that you've represented your favorites in one miniature landscape.

If you create a storybook-land, avoid attempting to show everything exactly as it was written (or shown on film). Instead, think about what you remember most while reading the book and what left the biggest impression on you. In *The Wonderful Wizard of Oz*, who comes to mind first—Glinda or the Wicked Witch? Choose one of these characters as your starting point. Would your Little Red Riding Hood be in the woods or at Granny's cottage? Brick, twigs, or straw—which material would you pick to make a house for three little pigs?

Whatever theme you decide on—whether it reflects a fairy tale, a garden style, everyday life, a memory, or a dream destination—you now have the foundation on which to build your garden. Remember: As many variations on garden themes exist as there are people who tend them. For your fairy garden creation, choose a theme that you love, and you can't go wrong.

Chapter 2

Designing with a Captivating Focal Point

The focal point of your fairy garden should capture the most visual interest. This main element to which the eye naturally falls is often (but not always) the largest ingredient of your miniature garden scene. Besides adding visual interest, the focal point instantly portrays the type of landscape you're creating. Choose a castle on which to base your landscape and the look you're striving for immediately becomes apparent. Of course, many variations on this particular fairy tale theme exist. A natural setting of trees, shrubs, and groundcover suggests a *Sleeping Beauty*–style castle situated in the mountains. Or give your fairy world the look of an European monarch dwelling with classic pathways lined with sand for "gravel" and neatly clipped hedges or rows of trees mimicking the geometric layout in Marie Antoinette's Versailles. You can even surround a castle with a moat made of blue aquarium gravel or crushed glass for added effect.

Mini-tip: Creating Clear Water

When making a body of water for your miniature garden, first put down a layer of small, white decorative rock before adding the blue glass or gravel. Installing this initial layer of white rock prevents the soil from seeping up and making the blue look muddy.

The best way to choose a focal point is to simply start with something you love. Design around a garden piece that complements the exterior of your home or choose the exact opposite for contrast. For example, if you live in a mid-century-style house but have always longed for a Victorian cutting garden, this is the perfect opportunity to create the landscaping of your dreams!

Birdhouse Centerpiece

Birdhouses make wonderful focal points and come in a wide variety of architectural styles. You may already have a few that you've used for indoor and outdoor display. Spring, when many craft stores and home and garden centers stock up on birdhouses, is the perfect time to choose a decorative one for your fairy garden. The key word here is *decorative*. A large majority of birdhouses are only for display and not intended for outdoor use. With this in mind, consider the following guidelines when selecting one for your garden.

Resin birdhouses fade slightly if placed in full sunlight, but they weather well. Porcelain birdhouses may sound fragile, but this material endures the elements, as does ceramic. You may want to use wooden houses, but look for ones without a lot of added décor, and before using, be sure to seal them with three to four coats of clear polyurethane spray. Avoid wooden birdhouses with glued-on faux flowers and whimsical items. They may be cute, but after coming in contact with water a few times, they will look like a hurricane hit! (Of course, if you live in an area prone to frost, protect your fairies and their homes by storing them away for the winter.)

Once you've found the perfect birdhouse, take a good look to determine its architecture. Does the house feature gingerbread accents of the Victorian era? Then decorate your garden with distinctive features of that time period, such as gazing balls, embellished pots and planters, fancy benches, and statuary. With your landscaping, imitate the Victorians' love of full, lush gardens by choosing complementary plants that offer a range of texture and coloration.

Perhaps your birdhouse resembles a rustic cabin. Substitute Adirondack chairs for iron benches, use furniture made from twigs, and add tiny animals to incorporate

a bit of wildlife. A cabin calls for trees and shrubs with a free-form, unclipped look to them. Create winding paths that meander off into the trees to suggest a newly blazed hiking path.

Great Little Gazebos

Architectural features make a strong focal starting point. The gazebo is a perfect example of a highly recognizable garden element. In days past, gazebos sat in the center of a city's park or town square and served as a meeting place for the community for band recitals, speeches, and general entertainment. In a contemporary setting, a gazebo offers the comfort of shade on a hot afternoon or an intimate

place to sit with friends and sip a drink. The beauty of including a gazebo in your landscape is the fact that it can be viewed from 360 degrees. While all fairy gardens have something to offer from every angle, most are planted to be viewed primarily from the "front" of the container. If you choose to plant a fairy garden for viewing from each side, leave room for plants all around the focal feature. It isn't necessary to put the gazebo (or focal object) directly in the center of the container, though. You can place it two-thirds of the way in and still have plenty of space to create your visuals. Think of the pot as a pie sliced into four pieces. As you plant and accessorize, be sure to include something of interest for the eyes to land on in each of the quarters, while continuing to direct the viewer to your focal image.

Mini-tip: Repurposed Gazebo

This gazebo—intended as a cake topper—was purchased at a craft store. Apply a few coats of white spray paint and it's ready to be the center of attention.

Archway Accents

A garden that highlights a simple archway as its focal point is one of the easiest to plant. Archways are especially useful if you've never ventured into any type of gardening before—miniature or otherwise. At the same time, such structures possess a classic elegance ideal for more complicated designs.

For the beginner, using the rule of symmetry is key. In other words, what you plant on one side of the archway you "mirror" by planting on the opposite side as well. Position the arch structure toward the back of the pot and center it. Choose a plant with stems long enough to cover the archway and put one on each side.

You can either weave the plant through the trellises or tie it to the structure with monofilament fishing line. Once complete, you will have a focal point seeming to support years of growth from your "vines." Next, choose two contrasting plants and place them on the left and right sides of the arbor's opening. (Depending on the size of your container, you can plant two or three different types of plants on each side.) Put some low-growing groundcover in front of these, leaving open space down the middle for your pathway. Then add a single plant at the very back to soften the view as you look through the archway. Other than the back plant, both the left and right sides of your garden should be mirror copies.

You can continue the formality of this planting and install matching pairs of pots or benches on either side of the path. Or you can let the archway act as a frame for your scene by placing something in the center of the arbor, such as a fairy sitting at a bistro table or on a stool.

While strolling through a life-size garden, you most likely encounter a number of focal points along the way. An angel statue at the heart of a rose bed, a birdbath in the midst of the herbs, or a jasmine-filled arbor at the end of a walkway—these all draw the viewer's eye. Often, each area, or "garden room," has one defining item that complements and completes the section in which it's displayed. This should also be the case when crafting your fairy garden landscape.

Using Focal Restraint

When working on your fairy landscape, the temptation to add loads of adorable miniatures can result in a garden that looks over-decorated. If you find that choosing just one piece as a focal point is difficult, always remember you can make more than one garden! Opt for clarity versus clutter. As you select your main object, stay true to your selected theme. A Medieval castle would seem sadly out of place next to a Victorian fountain, even if you do want them both. Instead, create just the right surroundings for each of the focal points in two separate pots.

When planting, avoid trying to capture an entire garden in one container. Instead, think of each landscape as a little corner of the world. The idea is for the viewer to enjoy your creation and mentally fill in what lies beyond. For example, looking at a scenario with a rocky path leading toward a beautiful fountain, your imagination can easily envision a grand estate in the distance. The "Fountain Garden" is not the complete picture, but rather a portion of the grounds that wind about a large manor house. Your fairy garden should be like attempting to take a picture at a park. If you try to get everything the park has to offer in one photo, nothing stands out because so much is vying for your attention. Focus your shot (your garden) on one standout feature, and you will succeed in representing the beauty of the park as a whole.

Even a garden that is meant to mimic nature can benefit from the addition of one primary focal element. A premade resin waterfall or one that's homemade from local rocks can be the start of a forest scene. Or what about surrounding that same waterfall with small ferns, ivies, and the tangled appearance of a jungle? The toy section in a store can yield a treasure trove of plastic or rubber animals to set amid the growth. A portion of a fallen tree limb or a

piece of driftwood becomes the entrance to Peter Pan's Neverland, and a wee cottage nestled among tiny pines beckons Snow White to the home of the Seven Dwarves.

Aquarium suppliers offer a vast supply of waterproof accent pieces. A fiberglass cave (originally intended for an iguana habitat) creates an ideal starting point for a rugged mountain scene. A readily available fish tank bridge spans a "river" created from blue craft glass. (Just a note: Anytime you create a river, make sure to dig a one-inch deep trench to hold the glass or rock. If you just sprinkle it on top of the soil, it washes away with the first rain or heavy watering.)

Do you have a favorite vacation spot near a lake or a much-loved campsite in the hills? Is there a place with gorgeous views that makes you feel peaceful every time you visit? Why not re-create a portion of that natural scenery in miniature. Next time you visit, look for one identifying feature and snap a picture of that part of the area. Use it as a reference guide to build your "Getaway Garden." If *you* have a spot that is perfect for picnics, no doubt your fairies will love it too!

Center of Attention

Usually, you'll want to display your delightful creation near a well-traveled path, such as a porch or patio, near a sitting area, or at the start of a walkway. This keeps your fairy garden close at hand for watering and the occasional pruning. Most of all, you'll want your fairy tale landscape nearby so friends and family can admire and enjoy it. If you decide to place a fairy garden deeper into the landscape, consider using a focal point in a lighter color tone. For instance, a white birdhouse or gated arbor pops out even in a shady spot. A bit of brightness in the distance draws attention and invites people to come take a closer look. After all, fairies hate to be ignored!

Your focal point can be as simple and natural as a tree. Open any gardening magazine and you'll find dozens of pictures showcasing vignettes under the sheltering branches of mature trees. A weeping willow at the water's edge, a slender Italian cypress flanking a wall fountain, a shady spot to rest under a maple—the beauty of trees softens the horizon and blurs the concrete edges of our cities. It would be difficult to find any true gardener who didn't have at least one tree growing in the yard, no matter how small.

Choosing the right mini tree for your garden reinforces the style for which you're striving to obtain. Cryptomeria, junipers, conifers, and cypress lend softness to the landscape in keeping with a mountainous or forested look. Single-trunked trees created from plants such as boxwood, cuphea, myrtle, or serissa are perfect candidates for backyard specimens highlighted with low-growing plants underneath.

Resources for fairy trees are as close as your local nursery or garden center. Even if they don't stock miniature plants, a bit of detective work can reveal a perfect candidate. Look at the shrubs in one-gallon containers. What you want is something that would normally grow to not more than three feet tall. Believe it or not, with occasional pruning, many such plants can be kept to a height of 10 to 12 inches. Find a plant that has some texture to the main stem to simulate bark. A common plant that easily achieves this look is Rosemary prostrata. To prune rosemary into a "tree," cut off the lowest branches until you have a length of exposed "trunk" anywhere from 4 to 8 inches tall. Next, prune the upper growth so that it has a slightly rounded look. You don't want it to resemble the lollipop trees we all drew as kids, so make it look natural by thinning a few branches here and there. When you're finished, the top growth of the tree should equal one-third to one-half of the overall height of the tree.

Conventional planting advice teaches you to never purchase a root-bound plant that has roots coiled around the outside of the root ball, because the plant will forever remain stunted. For the purposes of fairy gardens, you actually want stunted, root-bound shrubs with branches and trunks that look gnarled or aged. So, scour the nursery for shrubs that have passed their prime.

A garden focal point doesn't have to be the biggest, the grandest, or the most expensive item in your garden. Sometimes it's just a simple piece that helps tell the story of your theme. A little metal bench can be the catalyst for an entire garden. What else can you add? Perhaps a sitting fairy looking down at her puppy; or glue a kitten on the bench and position a bird on top of the backrest.

Maybe you will perch a little boy fairy on the arm of the bench and put a teensy frog on the seat next to him. Think about the background, too. Some dark green trees and variegated shrubs would make the scene really stand out. Why not hang a little tire swing from one of the trees. What else can you include to show what a little boy would have in his yard? Perhaps a shovel next to a small hole that he's dug, or a wagon filled with sticks, toys, or even bunnies. Focal point choices are unlimited, so let your imagination soar!

Once you've decided on a theme and have selected your focal feature, take a moment to really think about how you want your fairy garden to look and what sort of story you want to convey. When this task is accomplished, you're ready to begin accessorizing your miniature landscape.

Chapter 3

Accessorizing Your Miniature Landscapes

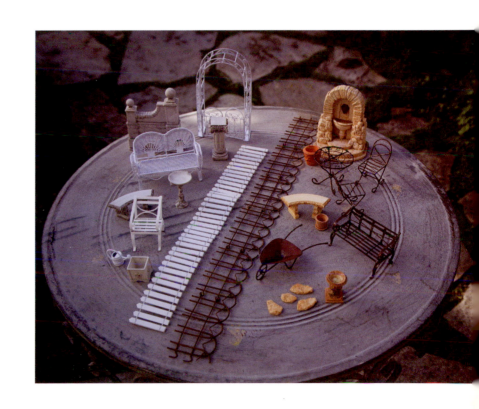

In the fashion world, accessories make the outfit. The same can be said for your fairy garden. Accessories visually support and enhance the theme or style of your miniature world and for that reason careful selection is important. A formal bench or pedestal would look completely out of place in a natural meadow setting. Likewise, you probably won't find gorilla or elephant figures hulking behind a picket fence! Domesticated pets like dogs and cats would be a better choice for that suburban scene.

As you select your accent pieces, try to keep them all in a similar color range. For instance, if your focal point is a rusty arbor, look for fencing in a rust, brown, or earth tone. Other great additions to this color scheme include pots and chairs with a warm tint—like beige or terra-cotta—brick paths, clay stepping stones, and sand. A white arch requires the cool colors of gray, silver, or charcoal, as well as the brightness of varying shades of white. Of course, mixing warm and cool colors isn't the end of the world, but doing so won't give you the same degree of design. A jolt of primary color can liven up a simple planting, but use it sparingly and balance boldly colored items with more neutral tones.

Mini-tip: Accessorizing with Sand

Use sand to achieve a number of looks, including a stretch of beach, a desert scene, or a dry-creek bed (when mixed with gravel). A thick layer of sand creates an impressive formal walkway. When purchasing sand, though, be certain that it is horticultural grade. Common playground sand sold at home supply chain stores is unwashed, which means it contains a lot of salt that could burn or otherwise damage your plants.

A number of fantastic online resources for accessories exist (many are listed at the back of this book). If your local nursery doesn't carry fairy minis, check hobby shops, dollhouse suppliers, or model railroad stores, as they always stock small-scale items that can be used for a miniature garden.

The holidays, besides being an anticipated time of year, bring loads of opportunities for miniature shopping. Christmas tree decorations come in a wide range of materials. Look for items with garden themes made from resin, metal, and wood. Tiny toys, like bikes and wagons used during the season for wreath decorating, show up in the ornament section year after year. Heart-shaped plastic picks used to adorn Valentine's Day cupcakes make a charming addition to a tiny flower bed. Insert a pick into the fairy garden scene as a decorative garden "stake," or enjoy lots of goodies and you have enough picks to edge a walkway!

Mini-tip: Seasonal Décor

Seasonal figurines can replace a fairy if you want to completely change the look and tone of your garden.

Mini-tip: Adding Holiday Cheer

Just wrapping "lights" around the arbor would be enough, but holidays are a time for indulgence—so add as many decorations as you like!

Accessory Options

Landscapers define a project by using two categories: softscaping and hardscaping. Softscaping refers to all of the plant materials, including trees, bushes, flowers, and lawns. Hardscaping comprises all the stationary elements that create the outline of the garden, including fencing, walkways, raised planters, pots, pergolas, gazebos, ponds, and poured patios. Unless you want a completely natural look, it's important to include at least one of the latter elements in your miniature garden. Fit in hardscape where the items would logically go. If you have an arbor, create a path leading up to it and beyond. What you put on either side of the walk should tie in with the theme and focal point and maintain your overall color scheme. A white arbor with an

antique flair beautifully complements a bench in a similar style, as well as a sundial or a statue.

Some companies offer fairy garden kits or pre-cast planters. If you feel insecure about making initial choices, these kits can be a lovely way to begin. Don't feel pressured to include everything they give you in the kit, however. And don't think you're cheating if you decide to add other items into the mix. When augmenting what the kit contains, look for miniature accessories in the same tonal family. A house surrounded by a low wall of faux rock rises

to a higher level of design when you add hardscaping in a muted palette of earth tones, such as a chocolate-brown fence enclosing the property, rustic stepping stones, and terra-cotta pots flanking the front door. Is it necessary to add these items to the garden? No, but such additions give your fairy world a more complete look and put your personal stamp on a manufactured piece.

Creating a fairy garden that reflects your tastes and interests makes it unique. Do you have a dog or cat? Include a mini replica of your pet as you accent the scene. When making a fairy garden as a gift, adding a miniature version of the recipient's four-legged family member is a guaranteed winner. Another way to easily personalize your garden is to create a sign such as: GRANDMA'S GARDEN, THE VANCES' VEGGIE PATCH, or FRIENDS GATHER HERE. Trim a Popsicle stick to the desired length. (Don't you just love projects that require the eating of a treat in order to get the raw materials?) Then paint the stick a coordinating color and use a fine-point permanent marker to write your saying.

Big Mini Decisions

Like the eternal conundrum of the chicken or the egg, our question is: Which comes first, the fairy or the chair? Do you start by choosing your fairy and then your accessories, or the other way around? There is no set answer for this, as both are viable options. Say you have all of your accent pieces and one of them is a wicker bench. That might steer you toward using a fairy in a sitting position; or a gated fence could prompt you to select a fairy that looks as if she's ready to walk through the opening. The reverse is also true. If you have a sitting fairy, then you require a chair or bench for her to sit on. Either method works well.

The biggest problem is deciding which fairy to use out of dozens, even hundreds, of choices out there! (All of the fairies shown in this book are from a company called Add An Accent, but there are numerous sources available, which are given in the back of the book.) Considering that your fairy will inhabit the wonderful world you are making, wouldn't it be fun to find a wee version of yourself? Or of your kids, grandkids, or best friend? Of course, there's nothing wrong with selecting a fairy simply because you love it! When in doubt, a great guide is to choose a fairy that matches the dominant color in your garden. If you feature two fairy figurines, a pair dressed in outfits of a similar tone present a harmonious look.

Found Treasures

Don't be embarrassed if you catch yourself raiding the kid's toy chest for tiny garden art. Everyday objects can be transformed with just a bit of imagination. Keep an open mind as you go through the junk drawer (admit it—we all have one!). That refrigerator magnet from a decade's-old trip can be attached to a metal fence in front of some plants and suddenly it's a fabulous plaque. How about the swizzle stick you saved from a memorable vacation? Many are topped with an animal or interesting shape and can be used as adorable yard stakes.

Ever done any remodeling? Go on a scavenger hunt through the garage or shed for remnants of old projects. That leftover tile from the kitchen black splash you saved "just in case" can be repurposed into a fairy patio. A single 6-inch tile becomes an outdoor entertainment area. Squares of tiles 2 inches or less in size lend the look of custom hardscaping. Leave the tiles on the mesh or install them individually with a little space in between. The latter method adds authenticity, because it allows for a bit of greenery to creep in between the tiles.

Often, trash is just garbage, but sometimes it's the start of patio furniture in Fairyland. Examine items headed for the trash or recycle bin. That clear plastic liter bottle could easily be a pond by cutting 2 to 4 inches off the bottom and sinking that portion into the soil until the cut edge is level with the surrounding groundcover. Fill the liner with water, and your pond is ready to be splashed in by miniscule ducks and frogs.

Take time to celebrate life. Pop open a bottle and save those champagne corks, which make fabulous itty-bitty stools. Once corks are released from the bottle, their bottoms expand and create a mushroom shape. Such fairy furniture is waterproof and just the right scale. Celebrate twice, and you'll have a pair! While you're enjoying life, order in a pizza or two for delivery. The plastic riser used in the center of the pizza to keep the cheese from sticking to the lid of the box makes a nice end table when set next to a 3-inch-high chair.

Mini-tip: Attach Items with Fast-Acting Glue

To secure objects to one another, such as a teacup to a table, use fast-acting adhesive glue. Such glues are comprised of cyanoacrylate, which withstands watering and other outdoor elements like sun, heat, and cold. Keep accessories in place by gluing golf tees, nails, or screws to their base and inserting into the soil.

Adapting Everyday Items

Small container lids with holes punched or drilled through for drainage transform into miniature pots and planters. Or save those flat screw-tops from bottles of water and use them as stepping stones. Any old baskets lying around? A round-shaped basket that is 12 inches or less in diameter becomes a delightful rustic fairy house. Remove any handles, turn the basket upside down, and cut out a small doorway— *voila!* Your very own fairy house.

If your idea of Fairyland is one found at the leaf-carpeted floor of the forest, take your imagination for a walk. Use nature's discards as the building materials for a pixie's palace. A stroll around the neighborhood or through your own yard yields countless raw ingredients.[1] Wire together twigs for a fence or trellis. Use

[1] Never pick items from public spaces unless you check in advance that it's ok to do so.

thimble-size pine cones glued on top of sticks for fence posts or as markers on a path. Flat-sided stones pressed into the soil make great stepping stones. Acorn caps serve as fairy bowls sitting atop a table made of bark. And curving trails edged with seashells or beach glass complement gnarled furniture cut from driftwood.

For those living in the heart of the city with nature nowhere in sight, use manmade items with an organic look. Likely additions to your garden landscape are readily available resin mushrooms in all shapes and sizes and birdhouses that include the earthy look of flowers, fruits, toadstools, and acorns. These oversize pieces lend a touch of whimsy and give fairy figures a childlike appearance.

Discover your hidden Michelangelo and try sculpting some accessories. Craft stores carry several types of modeling clay, which can be baked in the oven. The clays come in a rainbow of colors and once hardened are impervious to water. Start with something easy, such as Easter eggs to hide in your fairy garden in the springtime or pumpkins for the fall. Decorating for holidays and special occasions expands the enjoyment of your garden. Some well-placed holiday additions can completely transform the scene you've created.

As you can see, the options are limitless when it comes to accessorizing. Keep your eyes and imagination open, and you're likely to find the perfect additions to your miniature world.

Mini-tip: Decorating for a Birthday Bash

Exchanging the tea set for the cake is an easy way to decorate for a birthday. A few added balloons and you're ready for a party. If you plan to change out accessories, be sure you don't glue them in place. A touch of putty or earthquake hold will keep items temporarily secure and able to be replaced.

Chapter 4

Creating Action

One of the joys of gardening comes not just from the gorgeous roses or nodding spikes of delphiniums, but when visitors come to call. Nothing is quite so satisfying as seeing butterflies and hummingbirds zooming through your carefully tended plants. Watching children playing in the dappled sunlight and seeing the cat slink across the lawn elevates the garden from a pretty living picture to a wondrous environment meant to be shared. A garden never truly has a heart until it is filled with family, friends, pets, and wildlife.

This is also true for your fairy garden. While we can't shrink the kids and pets to wander along the tiny trails (although that would be fun!), there are many ways to create the illusion of life in our miniature landscapes. Of all the aspects of building a fairy garden, creating action is the most overlooked step. Everyone becomes so enchanted with the Lilliputian trees and plants and the tiny accent pieces and fairies that they forget the most important aspect—giving the illusion that someone (or something) actually lives in and enjoys the garden.

The secret to creating action in your fairy garden is to give viewers the "idea" of movement, which catches the eye and imagination. Plopping a figure in the middle of a planter isn't enough. What creates the illusion of movement is having the fairy relate to her environment.

Fairies on the Fly

One of the easiest ways to put action into your garden is to capitalize on the positioning of your fairy figurine. Is she "walking" forward? Placing her on a path leading away from an arbor gives the impression that she's out for an afternoon stroll. Glue a 6-inch twig in her hand to look like a staff and suddenly that stroll becomes the beginning of a hike through the hills. Add an extra spark of life in the tableau and have the fairy interact with other fairies or creatures. Or take that same fairy and this time have her heading toward something. Just by adding three little ducks opposite the fairy, you not only create action, but an entire scene suddenly comes to life. Now the viewer sees a fairy rushing to greet her dear friends from next door!

Mini-tip: Fairies in Motion

Gluing your fairy onto a mobile toy, such as a bicycle, indicates movement.

You can use the simplest "movement" to create a scene. Positioning even a seemingly static figure can transform the landscape into one teaming with life. If the fairy is sitting, perch her on top of a fence, the steps leading up to her house, or attach her to a bench. Then take it a step further. Are her arms raised? Glue an animal into her hands so that she appears to hold a beloved pet. Study the body language of the fairy and use the magic of "fairy focus." If she's looking up, put something or someone for her to gaze upon. If she's sitting on a chair under a tree, have her peering into the foliage. With every garden you create, get at eye level and follow the fairy's gaze. By always placing something for her to view, you guarantee action by seeing how she relates to her surroundings.

Animals in Motion

In addition to the "fairy focus," maximize your action potential by using the positioning of figures to create more movement. Adding tiny animal figurines to the garden is a popular way to suggest action. The key is where and how you place them. A young kitten wired onto a branch puts instant movement into the garden. Does your landscape have a pond? If so, think of ways that animals could interact with the water. Start, for instance, by placing a swan in the middle of the pond. Add another swan inches from the water's edge, making it appear as if the graceful bird is heading over to join its mate. Position a dog on the other side of the pond. Now you not only portray the suggested movement of two swans, but you also have the potential action of the dog chasing them both! Fish swimming in the pond might be an obvious choice, but amp up the storyline by inviting a sauntering horse to stop by for a drink. A little boy riding bareback gives you triple the action. (Notice that the fairy pictured on page 60 is the same one as in the photo on page 58. You can use all of these figures in myriad combinations.)

Place a little birdbath in your garden and then glue a bird to its edge, which automatically gives the idea of movement. Create even more action by setting a cat to spy on the bird from underneath a nearby shrub. By combining different animals in one garden, you set the stage for a little bit of fun conflict. Like the dog chasing the swans, the cat stalking the bird translates into action. While some animal figurines are made to look as if they're in motion, others are static. Don't let that stop you. Creating movement is easy—simply add another creature into the mix. For example, a deer standing with its head down may at first seem stationary, but follow the deer's gaze and place a bunny looking up at him. Suddenly the two are having their own private conversation.

Mini-tip: Suspending Birds and Butterflies

To hang creatures like birds and butterflies from taller items like trees or gazebos, and to create the illusion of flight, use thin-gauge (26–28) clear monofilament fishing line. This nearly invisible string is used in movies for special effects when objects need to look as if they are floating in thin air. No CGI animation needed!

Just as we did with the fairies, studying the body language of our critters inspires a mini tableau. In the photo on page 61, mama and baby goose started this tender scene. Using the action of the baby's inclined head, a watering can was inserted to look as if he's helping himself to a drink. Mama in the background watches carefully to make sure he's safe. The only movement here is a slight bend of the neck, and yet it becomes the catalyst for a sweet garden story.

Impending Action

Creating the promise of movement in your miniature garden also works well. This entails tricking the mind and eye. A rambunctious little boy glued to the outer corner of a low wall might be ready to leap off into the grass below. Just because your fairy is sitting, you aren't locked into putting him on a seat. If his arms are raised, glue a length of twine between his hands for a rope swing. He may not actually be in motion, but it looks as if he will be at any moment.

Using your accessories to portray upcoming action is another great avenue to pursue. A wheelbarrow full of soil and a small rake leaning against a fence show the intention of a bit of yard work. A twig ladder propped next to a birdhouse can mean holiday decorations will soon go up if your fairy holds a wee string of lights. Glue a thin twig with dental floss tied to the end in your fairy's clenched fist and you know that a fishing expedition is about to begin! Something as stationary as a tea set can become the hub of activity. A teacup tilting precariously on the edge of a tiny wrought-iron table teases you into expecting the worst. Add some animals into the mix and you have an impending tea party disaster.

Evidence of Action

The "footprints" we leave behind help the mind of viewers to conjure up an image of what happened before they arrived. Sticky fingerprints on the fridge may be a clue as to where the last of the dessert went. If you live on the coast, sand in the doorway suggests the remnants of a day at the beach. That overturned chair and plant stand might be the reason the kids are out of breath and the dog is panting. If the door to the shed is open, chances are someone has been in there. Even if no one is in sight, these tell-tale signs convey the message that somebody was recently around.

A mini mailbox with a door that can be opened, a tiny garden gate left ajar, a bicycle lying on the ground—these all imply some sort of previous action. Something as simple as a fairy looking at a pot lying on its side can speak volumes if you put a sad-eyed basset hound nearby. Did you see him knock it over? No. Do you know that he did it? Yes. In your mind's eye, you see a re-enactment of the accident and that translates into action.

Again, you can use the positioning of your fairy to help generate evidence of action. A little girl lifting the hem of her dress could have been trying to keep it dry as she waded through water. Or, stand the same fairy beneath a cotoneaster tree, place a few berries in her skirt, and now you have the charming scene of a sun-dappled afternoon spent picking apples.

Reflecting Movement

Including something that reflects movement works nicely to add action to your fairy garden. Not only do tiny gazing globes lend a Victorian cutting garden feel to the landscape, but they also catch the sun's rays and reflect passersby, birds, and the sway of nearby plants. Ponds and streams also lend sparkle while mirroring the breezy movement of the tiny trees above. Real water is a wonderful resource, as those ripples on the surface reveal the presence of visiting bees, ladybugs, or the hands of young family members doing some dabbling! If including real water isn't practical or desirable, create the illusion of running water with blue-tinted resin. Use this material to make life-like lakes and ponds or to fill fountains and birdbaths.

Creating action in the garden helps you set the stage for the most important part of constructing a fairy garden: telling a story.

Chapter 5

Telling a Story

What part of childhood could be sweeter than lying in bed listening to Mom or Dad read a favorite story? With every turn of the page, your mind conjures up images more vivid than any illustrator could create. As an adult, how many times have you eagerly awaited the film version of a much-loved novel, only to leave the theater feeling cheated because the on-screen adaptation failed to live up to what you envisioned while reading? Our imaginations excel at taking small bits of information and inflating stories into larger-than-life versions. This same concept holds true when friends and family admire your fairy garden.

With a well-designed miniature garden, the theme, fairies, and accessories combine to convey your specific tale, while still allowing viewers to see the story of their imagination. Just as a painting affects two people differently, fairy gardens are open to multiple interpretations.

In the photo on the opposite page, what do you notice first? Is it the fairy flying the kite or the puppy trying to capture the end of the string? Eventually, you'll discover every detail of the scene, but that first impression determines the story the garden tells you.

In the last chapter, you learned the importance of creating action in your fairy landscape. Now, by setting the scene and learning how to tell a tale, you take your garden to the next level. While action is the result of having your fairy relate to her surroundings, the story comes from how she reacts to that world.

Let's say you've selected a fairy in a sitting position for your garden tableau. Positioning her on the edge of a bench starts the action. Using the fairy focus method requires placing something for her to gaze down upon. What we choose to put in her line of vision influences the storyline. A watering can suggests the fairy is taking a break from her gardening chores. Is she eager to get back to work? If the answer is

yes, gluing a garden trowel in one hand implies that she's taking a quick rest and will soon jump right back into planting. If the answer is no, a cup of tea on the bench beside her suggests a lazy afternoon spent procrastinating. Two different accessories; two different tales. Instead of the watering can, position an animal figurine at her feet. Now the story has nothing to do with gardening—it's about a fairy having a lovely chat with her dog.

Surprising Twists

As we discovered in Chapter 4, using impending action is an effective way to start a scenario. Next, try adding something unexpected. A garden featuring a bird clinging to the seat of a bike can be titled LEARNING TO RIDE if you have a fairy standing with her arms out in front of the handlebars ready to steady a potential fall. Or, instead of the usual cat stuck in a tree, try a teddy bear. Place a fairy below holding up her skirt ready to catch him and an audience of frogs, squirrels, and ducks all breathlessly watching a rescue worthy of the fire department. Tuck a pig inside a dog house with a terrier anxiously peering inside. In the background, a fairy carries a dish of dog food to the scene. What do you think happens next? This is where your imagination fills in the rest of the action and tells the story.

While including many types of animals creates interesting conflict and spices things up, highlighting animals of the same kind or breed invites an endearing look at families. For instance, a kitten walking along a garden wall is cute on her own, but even more precious when mama purrs encouragement from below to the last of her litter.

Babies are always a favorite subject matter and a catalyst for the most heartwarming of stories. Get magical results by pairing a baby fairy and baby animal. For a family scene, have a big sister instigate the action by pulling a wagon containing her little sister and a duckling. Or seat that same baby on the back of a very patient golden retriever. Follow her focus and have the retriever pup wagging his way toward them.

The viewer may wonder if the pup is coming to greet his best pal. Maybe both babies are ready for naps under Mom's protective watch. Or perhaps the pup is announcing a party at the hedgehog's house next door. By using the two dogs and fairy child, you set the scene. How the story reveals itself is up to the viewer's imagination.

Compelling Symbols

Some images are so iconic there is no need for embellishment. One glance at the Statue of Liberty and you know the setting is New York. Likewise, a picture of the Eiffel Tower creates an immediate sense of place. If you decide to build a garden around a well-known theme or idea, there is no need to add on to the storyline because of its enduring reputation.

Is there a more recognized symbol of fairy tales than that of the beautiful maiden and her frog prince? Most of us have known the ending to this storybook romance since youth. In creating your own version, remember to use the aspects of the story that stand out to you in particular. Perhaps you depict their "meeting" next to a sun-dappled pond. Or maybe you create a scene on a forested pathway as the maiden walks to the center of town. It doesn't matter if the backdrop is a castle, a cottage, or a gated wall. What's important is showcasing the key elements of the tale—the girl and the frog.

While fairy tales work well, a vignette can also stem from very ordinary, everyday situations. Sometimes such real-life scenes are the most charming of all, because they offer a snapshot of everyday life. A little boy standing on a chair to peer over a fence sparks all kinds of ideas. Who or what is he looking at? Is there an older brother or sister holding the back of the chair to prevent a fall?

Even daily chores become the basis for poignant little stories. A morning spent watering the yard is a fairly common task. Just by having your fairy standing near some shrubs with a mini hose, you show viewers an activity with which they are familiar. A sweet-faced German shepherd sitting next to the fairy provides something for her to look at, but the empty water bowl at the dog's paws really tells the tale.

Meaningful Chatter

If you're unsure about finding your fairy garden story, remember you can't go wrong with a pleasant conversation. Simply position two figurines so they face each other. It could be two fairies, one fairy and an animal, or two animals. One of the conversationalists can even be a tree, as seen in the photo at the beginning of this chapter. A "live" bear or a "stuffed" teddy—either one works. Remember, this is Fairyland and anything is possible! Dogs can talk, cats can sing, and trees can tell stories.

When interior designers decorate a room, they use the technique known as "layering." First, they decide which style best suits their client, be it Modern, Traditional, Tuscan, or so forth. Next, they concentrate on wall coverings and painting, and then they add the rugs, furniture, and lighting fixtures. The final step consists of lamps, photos, pillows, artwork, and accessories. When the designer finishes, the once-empty room transforms into a space in which people want to gather. A good designer layers in enough detail to not only reflect the owner's tastes, but to give a sense of his or her personality. In other words, the room tells a story about who lives there. You can do the same with your fairy garden landscape.

Mini-tip: Creating a Kite

Create a kite from ordinary objects found around the house. Cut a bright lid of a container of cleaning wipes into a kite shape with scissors. Glue a tail cut from a length of plastic garden tie onto a piece of dental floss and adhere to the kite's bottom. All of the elements are waterproof, and the kite will last for years. Tell a story and give the impression that the kite is flying by loosely tying the top of the kite to a tree branch.

Every step you've learned so far is a layer of your finished fairy garden.

In the picture opposite, consider each of the elements. A suburban backyard is the theme and the beautiful cypress tree is the focal point. With white as the main color, accessories include a doghouse, a wheelbarrow, and a birdhouse. The fairy stands still, so keeping the wheelbarrow directly in front of her implies action. The story comes from the beagle puppy eager for a ride and the pup's mom, who urges the fairy pushing the wheelbarrow to "Please go slowly!" All of the design layers work together to tell our captivating fairy tale.

Chapter 6

Planting and Care Practicalities

Before you begin selecting plants, decide where you wish to place the fairy garden. In the sun or in the shade? For the most part, we identify sun plants as needing direct sun for six hours or more each day. The definition of shade includes areas that get morning but no afternoon sun, bright indirect light, or filtered sun throughout the day. There are some climate exceptions to consider as well. In desert areas, for example, plants termed as needing full sun often require a bit of protection during the hotter times of the year. If you live where snow and frost are the norm in winter, protect your fairy garden or consider using small-scale, easily replaced annuals each year. Don't panic if you have no experience planting, though! A trip to a local nursery will help you understand what plants are available and well suited for your growing region.

The gardens featured in this book are for outdoors only. You could certainly bring one inside to use as a centerpiece for an evening, but move it back outside as soon as the last party guest pulls out of the drive. These fairy gardens aren't meant to stay indoors for more than a few hours and even at that, only a couple of times a year. But is it possible to create a fairy garden for indoors? Yes, but plant choices are very limited. You can use houseplants, but it's difficult to find any that stay within the scale in which we are working.

Nearly Unlimited Options

Online growers offer a dazzling array of miniature conifers and junipers. Before you think of ordering, check to see if they are compatible with your climate zone. Fantastic sources for miniature plants are nurseries and growers that cater to model railroaders and bonsai enthusiasts. Finding a supplier in your immediate area is ideal, as such acclimated plants are sure to thrive in your garden. Plants don't have to be truly miniature in order to work, either. Even commonplace herbs fit well in a 1:12 scale. Curly-leaved parsley can be trimmed as a hedge, and thyme comes in numerous varieties and colorations. This herb works particularly well due to its diminutive leaf size. As you look for plant material, inspect the leaves and consider if the foliage is small enough to be convincing in a miniature setting.

When designing a standard flower bed, the rule is generally to start high and end low. Taller trees and shrubs go toward the back, midsize bushes and flowers in the middle, and low-growing border plants at the front. This guideline works nicely for mini gardens as well. Trees should be somewhere between 8 and 18 inches tall. Anything higher than that begins to overwhelm the scene. Mid-range bushes should be kept to 6 inches or less, and the lowest height is reserved for the fairy equivalent of grass. While there are many groundcover varieties from which to choose, it's important that your selection really hugs the ground. Some plants sold as groundcovers reach up to 7 or 8 inches high, which means your fairy must wade through 8-foot-tall grass!

Contrast Is Key

As you look for plant selections, seek out combinations that feature a variety of textures, such as the frothy growth of a cypress paired with a needlelike pine or the flat, oval leaves of a mini olive tree next to a softly branched juniper. The juxtaposition of hard and soft and dark and light tones creates visual interest. Such contrast also gives the impression of variety, making the garden seem full with only a few plants. Coloration and tonal shades are also very important. Just adding one plant in bright yellow or chartreuse can make everything around it look better because of the contrast. If you use three plants that are the same tint of green, you can hardly tell one from the other at a short distance away. Giving the garden that one pop of contrast—whether it's lime, gray, or even a lighter green—provides the interest you need.

How many flowers are in a garden? Once you start scaling the plantings down, you'll find it doesn't take many blooming plants to convince the eye that the flower bed is full. You don't even need blooms to create this effect. Vivid leaves like the "Pink Splash" *Hypoestes* brighten a shady spot and give the suggestion of a floral hedgerow. A blooming groundcover, like isotoma or wooly or one of the various creeping thymes, make a lovely show in spring and summer when in flower but still look good when just a carpet of greenery. One single blossoming tree sets the stage for admiring glances all through the season and doesn't necessarily need the competition of a flowering shrub.

Plants that get a little too tall or wide for use as a shrub have the potential to be a "vine" covering an arbor. Veronica (speedwell) has tiny flowers in varying hues of blue. The plant needs trimming more frequently than some, but the results are worth the effort. *Fuchsia thymifolia* is an anomaly. If left untended, it can leap to heights of 8 feet tall, but with monthly pruning it easily stays in scale. (If you have hummingbirds in your planting zone, this plant is one of their favorites. How charming to watch these birds flit through your fairy garden lured by the irresistible nectar!) Micro-needlepoint ivy is the most versatile of all and can be manipulated into any configuration. Look for plants with soft, flexible stems to curve over an arbor's arch.

Mini-tip: Succulent Additions

Small cuttings from sedums and succulents are a tremendous way to fill up an itty-bitty pot. If you can, drill a small hole in the little container. That way, the new planting will eventually take root into the fairy garden through the hole in the pot and won't need any special watering. Otherwise, expect to give the container a little drink every day in hot weather. The beauty of using these drought-tolerant plants is the fact that they can go totally dry in between. So if you miss a watering, they'll be fine. No need to wait for these cuttings to grow a root system—just snip and tuck them into a pot.

Time to Plant!

Once you've made your final selections, set your container on a table or someplace elevated so you can work on it at close to eye level. This really helps you monitor how all of the different elements are working together. The container you use must have at least one drainage hole. It is possible to plant in something with no drainage, but you must be extremely cautious about overwatering. If planting with no drainage holes, place a thick layer of gravel at the bottom before you add the soil so that excess water can pool below without the plant's root system staying constantly wet. Otherwise, the plants could easily rot. Remember that roots are like wicks. If they're touching water, they'll keep pulling moisture up, even if the plant doesn't need a drink. (Planting without drainage holes is definitely for more advanced gardeners.)

Keep soil in the container by placing a screen, a bit of broken pottery, or a small rock loosely over the drainage hole(s). You want the water to freely run through, but this helps to keep the dirt from eroding out over time. Because plants come in different size plastic pots, it is much simpler just to fill your container to the brim with soil. That way you can dig each hole to the depth that you need, like you would if planting in the ground. Use a high-quality potting soil (not a mulch), and avoid those soils with water-saving polymers, as they often retain water in an uneven manner. Place your chosen focal point in the proper spot, and you're ready to begin planting.

Mixing a time-released fertilizer into your potting soil at planting time is fantastic for starting your plants off right. After your initial planting, only feed with an all-purpose liquid fertilizer at half-strength if the foliage is looking pale or if you want to give the plants a nudge at the start of spring. Remember, you don't want things growing quickly!

As you plant, keep the top of the root-ball of each plant even with the rest of the soil. Nice and level is what you want. If you plant something a bit lower than the

others, all the water will run down to it and possibly keep it too wet. Also avoid planting anything higher than the other plants or it may dry out in warm weather. When adding groundcovers, you don't want the top of the greenery to match the soil level but the actual top of the root-ball instead.

Always tamp the soil firmly around and in between the root balls of each plant as you proceed. This not only keeps everything in place, but leaving air space or pockets between the plants can cause them to heat up in summer, which will damage the root system. When situating your plants, keep in mind the location of any intended path and leave that area open. If using a vining plant, don't attempt to weave or tie it to an arch until after you've watered.

Now that everything is planted, gently water until you see liquid running out of the bottom of the pot. This way, you'll know that the soil is completely saturated. Let the pot drain for a while and then go back and water again. Repeat three or four times. You will only give the fairy garden multiple waterings after you first plant. This is necessary because new potting soil is like a dry sponge, and it can take several soakings to get the moisture level consistent.

From then on, you will only water thoroughly once each time. A saucer underneath the pot isn't necessary or desirable, as trapped water may be pulled back into the container. Should you need a saucer to protect the surface where your garden is located, remove the excess water after every watering. (Using a turkey baster is a simple way to get the extra water out of the saucer if the pot is too heavy to move.)

Once the garden is saturated, scoop out the dirt where any pathways lead so you have a 1-inch-deep trench. Now when you add the rock or gravel, it will stay in place. If you use miniature brick, putting rock underneath makes for easy clean-up when it's time to trim back the groundcover. Simply lift the brick off and reset it again after the pruning. With pathways in place, tie the vines to the arbor and position your fairy and accessories.

Maintenance

It would be ideal if only one answer existed for the question, "How often to water?" A sun garden might need watering every day in summertime if temperatures soar, and as little as once every few weeks in winter. You want to keep the soil moist, but not soggy. Poke a finger into the top inch or so to see if it feels dry before you automatically break out the hose. If the pot accidentally goes so dry that some plants become limp, a thorough soaking should revive them. Such drought is not ideal, but plants often tolerate drying out once or twice without dying. You may lose some foliage and the plants won't look as robust for a while. Constant overwatering does far more damage than underwatering, though. If you're unsure, wait another day before watering and recheck for water readiness.

Trimming

Don't be afraid to trim! Usually you'll need to prune the sun gardens twice a month in summer and once a month in winter when the growth rate slows. Shade gardens need trimming about half as often, which amounts to once a month in summer and every other month in winter. The best way to determine when to give a "haircut" is anytime a plant starts to cross its boundaries or gets too tall. You'll find the groundcovers require pruning most often and the trees less so. In fact, some tree varieties don't need any pruning. Certain low growers, like baby's tears or isotoma, can be pruned almost to the ground and will bounce back in a few weeks, while Irish moss can never have the top growth trimmed—only the side growth to keep the paths clear. As you trim the trees, keep in mind that cutting just above a leaf joint or notch minimizes the amount of bare stem left behind, which gives a much cleaner look.

Fairies Love to Party!

A growing trend for girls' birthdays is fairy parties, where the guests plant their own little gardens. It can be expensive to furnish all of the ingredients of a fairy garden, but here are a few tips to help keep costs down.[2]

---

[2] Keep in mind that small children should always have adult supervision when working on their gardens.

Start with smaller pots—around 8 inches in diameter. This way, all you need is one tree or shrub and some groundcover to fill the garden. Look for low-growing groundcovers that are sold by the flat. One flat is enough for nine gardens if you leave space for pathways. In addition to the path, you'll need some sort of "hardscaping." Fencing cut or separated into small sections of about 4 to 6 inches in length provides just enough to give the garden some structure. Remember, we are avoiding that "fairy just stuck in a pot" look, so some type of accessorizing is needed. A bag of inexpensive plastic animals may not have the sophistication we normally give our gardens, but little girls enjoy choosing which one to add to their creation. Encouraging guests to come dressed as fairies provides an instant celebration and is a nice ice-breaker for kids who might not know each other well.

A favorite customer once shared a delightful secret with us. She bought an old metal mailbox (the kind with the red flag that can be raised for mail pick-up), painted it in girlish shades of purple and pink, and decorated the sides with a few sparkly "gems." Every time her granddaughter came to visit, the child raced to the mailbox to see if the fairies had left her any letters. Sure enough, they always did! The granddaughter wrote notes back to her fanciful pen pals, tucking them in the box when she left. Incorporating this approach into your party is a fun start. Give each guest a little fairy note and watch the magic begin.

Chapter 7

The Perfect Home:
Container Choices

The majority of fairy gardens are planted in low terra-cotta bowls about 16 inches in diameter. Several attributes make this type of pot so desirable. One of the main reasons such containers are used so often is their simplicity of design. They don't detract your attention—instead they put the emphasis on the garden itself. These containers are inexpensive, which is always a good thing. And you can move them around. Portability is particularly useful if the amount of sunlight your yard receives changes with the seasons. Your garden can literally follow the sun if placed in a portable container. To make viewing of shallow bowls easier, you'll want to elevate them on a small table, pedestal, or even a stack of cinderblocks.

When purchasing a terra-cotta bowl, try to find a kiln-fired American or Italian standard clay variety. While Mexican clay pots are cost-effective, they are set out in the sun to "cure," rather than being kiln-fired. This drying method leads to lightweight pots that only last a few years before breaking and crumbling. Many stores carry a plastic version of the low bowl and even offer them in a terra-cotta color. There's nothing wrong with using this type, but be careful moving it. Such pots have a flexibility that can cause the soil to shift in transit.

If you live in an apartment or condo, outdoor space can be at a premium. Using a hanging basket is an excellent solution to this problem. Such containers come in a wide variety of materials and styles and can be found in any nursery or garden center. Try matching the look of the container with the style of the fairy garden you plan to create. An ornately scrolled metal basket makes a nice companion for a Victorian planting, whereas the more natural look of willow, moss, or wicker pairs well with a cottage scene.

Limited space calls for taking advantage of every vertical inch possible. Hanging baskets are generally suspended from above with wires or chains. Seize the opportunity to add a little more pizzazz to your fairy garden by training tiny ivy or trailing plants to climb the chains or wires. This softens the harshness of the hardware and creates a frame for the view of the fairy garden.

Everything and the Kitchen Sink

A visit to thrift stores and flea markets provides inspiration for countless fairy gardens. Don't limit yourself to conventional ideas of planters. Almost any vessel with a depth of 3 inches or more works well. For M & M Nursery, one treasure hunt yielded an old sink in which we created a fairy garden. The fun factor kicked in when we added a re-circulating pump into one side of the garden and fed the tubing into the faucet so it "filled up" the sink for a dishwashing session. The pitcher and plates were purchased for next to nothing and when nestled into the sweet alyssum gave the appearance of sitting in soapsuds. A great argument for one man's trash is another woman's treasure!

A wonderful swap-meet find included an old chest of drawers. Several coats of polyurethane protected the exterior from constant waterings, and inside the drawers were painted with a layer of roofing tar after the drilling of several drainage holes. Pulling out the three drawers in stair-step fashion (with the bottom opened the widest) allowed for planting a garden in each one. Before adding the soil, bricks were inserted toward the back of each drawer to counterbalance the weight.

Old baker's racks are also a common find at secondhand stores. They make a great display stand for your garden and can often be incorporated into your theme. Plant a little tableau in a kitchen colander lined with moss to keep in the soil. On another shelf put a stock pot or enamel roaster containing a fairy garden (just make sure to drill drainage holes first). Hang a ladle from one of the shelves planted with a dollop of greenery and featuring a fairy sitting right on the edge. Several gardens combined into one setting and tied together by theme create a true fairyland from cast-offs.

From Ordinary to Extraordinary

Sometimes all it takes is a little help to turn the everyday into the extraordinary. At the nursery, we transformed a child's old metal bed into a quaint country theme by building a simple wooden box to sit on top of the frame (see opposite page). As it's only 4 inches deep, you might think the bed too shallow to support much growth, but everything in the photo was planted two years ago. The limited root space helps keep the plants from growing too fast, so the upkeep is truly minimal.

Mini-tip: Pixie Bench Basics

If something appears unusable because there is no planting area, think again. The flat surface of an old patio chair or table works beautifully as a one-of-a-kind container. Chicken wire can be used to form an edge and then filled in with sphagnum moss to contain the soil, or if the furniture piece has a mesh surface, wire onto the edge a 4-inch rim of a pot in order to create a plantable area. If the mesh in the seat is fairly large, line it with a thin layer of moss. Around a curvy bench, use flexible PVC bender board to create the rim. Metal rusts, so keep that in mind as you find a location for your newly made planter. A shabby chic chair garden stains concrete, so placement may be best on a lawn or at the front of a flower bed.

Tossing out beautiful garden ornaments once they pass their prime seems a shame. A cracked birdbath unable to hold water may no longer appeal to wildlife, but an entire fairy village gladly takes up residence. Improve drainage by using a tile or masonry bit to drill holes just above the joint where the bowl sits on the base. When landscaping a large-size basin, divide the container into three or four "slices," and each section can boast an individual scene.

Old fountains are often a source of guilt for people. Water restrictions in many cities force you to rethink that constant flowing water, or in many cases, they simply wear out or become damaged. Often you've paid way too much money to just throw a

fountain away, and yet you're at a loss as to what to do with it, so there it sits. Give the fountain a second life by planting a delightful miniature landscape inside, and

the former water feature can reclaim its place of prominence in the yard. Even wall fountains with their limited plantable space can be adapted to a lovely fantasyland.

Creative Cast-offs

An unusual wheelbarrow or wagon provides an excellent fairy garden container, as does a rusted-out bike. Make a charming statement by planting a fairy garden in the bike's handlebar basket. Speaking of baskets, grab that unused one from the back of the closet and blow off the dust bunnies. A tiny garden encased in a May basket looks charming—even in October. For durability, spray a few coats of paint on the outside of the basket. A glossy finish holds up far longer than matte. For best results, spray thin coats of paint to avoid drips, and let the basket dry completely between each application. Even if the basket is tightly woven, lining it with sphagnum or sheet moss is recommended to ensure the soil stays in place.

If you have room, an in-ground installation gives you enough space to satisfy every whim. Plant directly into the dirt after you have added a good mulch or compost. You want a fifty-fifty mix of half your existing soil and half mulch, down to a depth of 6 inches. If you have heavy clay soil, the deeper you prepare the soil the better. Some sort of raised edging is advisable to keep the garden contained and to define the boundaries. The only drawback is if heavy rains occur, because with a build-up of water, parts of the garden may wash away. So plan ahead and create small gullies to carry the water away from the garden.

The easier route is to use a raised planter (see opposite page), which can be made of brick, block, or pressure-treated lumber. A height of 16 to 24 inches makes for clear viewing and simple maintenance. Raised beds must be filled with potting soil. Mulch doesn't contain any actual dirt and is meant to be mixed with existing soil. Anytime you plant in a container (and a raised bed is essentially a large container), you need to use potting soil or potting mix that drains well.

Tiny Towns

If you've ever looked out the window of an airplane or seen an aerial photo of land below, you'll notice that the earth takes on the appearance of a green, crazy quilt. Trees, roads, and rivers are the "seams" that separate one patch from another. This is the perfect way to approach designing your large planter. Divide it into a number of different areas. How many depends on the size of the bed. One measuring approximately 6 by 8 feet requires a minimum of five, but no more than nine, different sections. Plant material can be used to create the borders, as well as fencing, walls, or other architectural features. In a large landscape, using contrasting plants is even more important so every segment has clear definition.

While you need an overall theme in a large fairy garden, each part can convey a different scenario. A public park, a backyard scene, and an approach to a cottage in the distance can all live in the same space. Accessories also help define each area, although it's still a good idea to keep them in the same color tones to maintain a unifying look.

A neat trick of the eye called forced perspective gives you the illusion of space on a grand scale. This little touch of magic works in a 16-inch container garden as well. When creating your garden, use our 1:12 scale from the front to the middle of

the planter. Then put slightly smaller accessories and buildings toward the back. The results of this technique can be seen when you try an experiment in the photos on page 108. Hold your hand over the picture, covering the larger bench on the right. With the bigger bench covered, the tiny cottage and smaller bench appear to be just a short distance from the front of the pot. Now remove your hand and look again. Placing the larger bench toward the front and the tinier one in the back makes the cottage seem further away.

Let's go through our checklist with this garden below. Our theme is an estate garden. Our focal point is the white arbor. Accessories are the statue, square pots,

watering can, and bench in the same cool tones as the arbor. Since two fairies are used, we keep them in the same shade of pink. Action is created by having one fairy rushing toward the gate and a second seated on the bench looking down. Our story is reinforced by the movement. The sitting fairy is focused on her beautiful dog, while the first girl runs to join her family and friends. Plant selections are simple. Isotoma showcases its white flowers in warm weather, surrounded by the green of micro-needlepoint ivy on the arbor and the Sophora tree in the background. The tricolor sedum in the pots that flank the arbor give the illusion of flowers and add contrast. And the container? The classic 16-inch terra-cotta pot.

The seven guidelines we've covered up to this point will help you discover the designer you've always suspected was inside of you. One of the joys of fairy gardening is how childlike we become when immersed in the hobby. Shake off the workaday world and open your imagination to all of the possibilities. You'll be surprised at how good you are at fairy gardening. There is only one true rule in gardening with miniatures, and that is to have FUN! Just be prepared. These gardens are like potato chips. It's almost impossible to have just one!

Chapter 8

Miniature Plants
for Fairyland

Thanks to the hybridizing efforts of plant specialists in recent years, a wide variety of miniature plants now exist for the fairy gardener. Many of the following plants are traditional favorites in diminutive form, while some are new plant selections. Find the following plants online and through your local independent nursery or garden center.

Low-growing Groundcovers (Sun)

Erinus Alpinus **'Dr. Hahnle or Hanle'**: Sometimes called fairy foxglove, this perennial evergreen alpine plant becomes covered in striking pink flowers from spring through summer.

Blue Isotoma (*Pratia/Isotoma fluviatilis*): Creeping perennial that forms a carpeting of tiny green leaves and starry blue flowers in spring and summer.

White Isotoma (*Pratia/Isotoma fluviatilis*): Creeping perennial that forms a carpeting of tiny green leaves and starry white flowers in spring and summer.

Lindernia grandiflora: Creeping groundcover with small bright green leaves. Grows no taller than 3 to 4 inches high. Covered in tiny white and purple snapdragon-like flowers spring through fall.

Mazus reptans: Perennial that grows 2 inches high and is covered by narrow, bright green leaves. In spring and early summer, the plant has purple-blue flowers with white and yellow markings.

Irish Moss (*Sagina subulata*): Perennial that creates an emerald-green carpeting of mossy, often mounded foliage. Sprinkled with small white flowers in spring.

Scotch Moss (*Sagina subulata aurea*): Golden green moss with mounded, undulating foliage.

***Silene uniflora* 'Druett's Variegated'**: Low-growing perennial with lance-shaped green and cream-colored foliage and white whorled flowers with prominent stamens.

Golden Stonecrop (*Sedum acre* 'Aureum'): Creeping groundcover with tiny light green succulent leaves. Stem tips turn yellow in spring. Golden, starry flowers cover the plant in summer.

Elfin Thyme (*Thymus serpyllum* 'Elfin'): Aromatic low-growing perennial herb with trailing stems and tiny round leaves. Plant grows 2 inches high by 5 inches wide.

Wooly Thyme (*Thymus pseudolanuginosus*): Perennial herb that creates a mat of wooly, gray, aromatic foliage.

Pink Chintz Thyme (*Thymus serpyllum* 'Pink Chintz'): Low-growing, one-inch-tall perennial herb with a compact growth habit. Covered in showy pink flowers in spring.

Red Creeping Thyme (*Thymus praecox* 'Coccineus'): Perennial herb that grows slowly to about 3 inches tall. Covered in lavender-red flowers during the summer.

Midsize "Shrubs" (Sun)

Armeria 'Nifty Thrifty': Perennial that reaches 4 to 6 inches tall with pink blooms. The plant's striking foliage is pale green edged in yellow.

***Armeria maritima* 'Rubrifolia'**: Perennial that reaches 4 inches high with hot magenta-pink flower heads in spring. Foliage turns burgundy-red in the winter months.

Chocolate Chip Bugleweed (*Ajuga x tenorii* 'Chocolate Chip'): A dwarf evergreen to semi-evergreen bugleweed with narrow, shiny, dark brown foliage and blue-stemmed flowers that rise above the foliage in spring.

Cuphea 'La Chiquita': Low-growing perennial that reaches 8 inches tall by 18 inches wide with a tight, dense growth habit. Features dark pink flowers spring through summer.

***Cuphea hyssopifolia* 'White Whiskers'**: Slow-growing evergreen shrub around 8 inches high. Has green foliage and white, starry summer flowers.

***Cuphea hyssopifolia* 'Compacta'**: Small, bushy evergreen plant reaches 8 inches high. Has glossy green leaves and dainty, tubular lavender-pink flowers.

***Erigeron karvinskianus* 'Spindrift'**: Graceful, low-growing, spreading perennial with delicate flowers that open white and fade to pink. May reseed.

***Erodium x variabile* 'Album'**: Mounding perennial with white, geranium-like flowers throughout the summer months.

***Erodium x variabile* 'Roseum'**: Perennial with a mounding growth habit that grows 3 inches high. Covered during the summer months with pink blooms veined in crimson.

Hebe Vernicosa: Compact shrub with a rounded growth habit and dark, glossy green leaves highlighted with yellow. The plant flowers in late spring with pale lilac blooms.

Christabel Hebe (*H.* 'Christabel'): Evergreen shrublet that reaches 5 inches high. Plant has yellow-green leaves and yellow stems.

Twiggy honeysuckle (*Lonicera nitida* 'Twiggy'): Dwarf honeysuckle with twiggy growth and yellow and green foliage. Fragrant creamy-white flowers in spring.

Pimelea prostrata: Low-growing shrub with blue-gray foliage. Features white flower clusters spring through summer.

Speedwell (*Veronica* species): Various flowers with eye-catching blooms in shades of white, pink, and blue.

Golden Thyme (various species): Perennial with yellow, lemon-scented leaves that grows 6 inches high.

Lime Thyme: Perennial shrubby herb that grows 6 inches tall. Features bright, lime-green foliage, a lemony fragrance, and pink flowers.

Silver Edge Thyme (*Thymus vulgaris* 'Argenteus'): Perennial herb with gray-green leaves edged in white. Lavender flowers cover the plant in summer. Grows 6 to 12 inches tall.

Tall "Trees" (Sun)

Dwarf English Boxwood (*Buxus sempervirens* 'Suffruticosa'): Small rounded shrub that creates tufts if left unpruned. Plant has lime-green foliage.

Variegated English Boxwood (*Buxus sempervirens* 'Aureovariegata'): Slow-growing boxwood with variegated green leaves edged with yellow-gold. Plant has mounded growth habit.

Morris Midget Boxwood (*Buxus microphylla Japonica* 'Morris Midget'): This aptly named miniature Japanese boxwood creates a rounded mass of bright green foliage. The plant grows an inch a year.

Justin Brouwers Boxwood (*Buxus sinica insularis* 'Justin Brouwers'): Compact mounded boxwood with small, deep green leaves.

Newport Blue Boxwood (*Buxus sempervirens* 'Newport Blue'): Dwarf mounding boxwood with stiff, upright branches covered in pointed, oval-shaped, blue-green foliage. Plant grows 3 to 5 inches per year.

Grace Hendrick Phillips Boxwood (*Buxus microphylla* 'Grace Hendrick Phillips'): Slow-growing boxwood with deep green, shiny foliage. Plant has a mounding growth habit.

Blue Dwarf Cypress (*Chamaecyparis pisifera* 'Dwarf Blue'): This miniature pyramid-shaped Sawara cypress has aqua-blue foliage.

Coprosma **'Rainbow Surprise'**: Dense, rounded shrub covered in green foliage with pale-yellow margins that turns from orange to red.

Coprosma **'Fire Burst'**: Small, evergreen shrub with eye-catching variegated foliage in green, pink, and cream.

Cotoneaster corokia: Often used in bonsai, this twiggy shrub features tiny fragrant flowers in spring followed by small scarlet berries.

Gray-Leaf Cotoneaster (*Cotoneaster glaucophyllus*): Gray-leaved small shrub covered by white flowers in the summer months that are followed by orange-red to red fruit that stay on the plant throughout winter.

Thyme-Leaf cotoneaster (*Microphyllus thymifolius*): Compact evergreen shrub featuring tiny leaves with rolled edges. Branches are dense and spreading, and the plant produces white flowers and red fruit.

Boulevard Cypress (*Chamaecyparis pisifera* '*Cyano-Viridis*'): Slow-growing dwarf cypress with fine-textured silver-blue foliage.

Compact Bronze Hinoki Cypress (*Chamaecyparis obtusa* 'Pygmaea Aurescens'): Slow-growing, mounded shrublet with yellow-bronze foliage in spring that changes to green in the summer and coppery-bronze during the winter months.

Hokkaido Chinese Elm (*Ulmus parvifolia* 'Hokkaido'): This slow-growing elm tree has medium-green foliage and grows no taller than 18 inches. It has the smallest leaf of all elms and is often used in bonsai.

Catlin Elm (*Ulmus parvifolia* 'Catlin'): Slow-growing elm that is often grown as a bonsai. Plant has shiny, tiny, dark green leaves.

Franke Bornmueller's Fir (*Abies bornmuelleriana* 'Franke'): This dwarf Turkish fir cultivar is evergreen and only grows 3 inches per year. It has medium-green dense foliage.

Shimpaku Fudu Juniper (*Juniperus chinensis* 'Fudu'): This dwarf blue juniper is often used for bonsai. Responds well to pruning. Grows 4 to 6 inches a year.

Shimpaku Juniper (*Juniperus chinensis*): A dwarf, upright growing juniper commonly used for bonsai. The plant has dark green, dull foliage and short, leafy branches.

Dwarf Japanese Garden Juniper (*Juniperus procumbens* 'Nana'): This common bonsai selection is a slow-grower perfect for container growing. The plant's new growth is green, turning to a bluish-green.

Sargent's Juniper (*Juniperus chinensis* 'Sargentii'): Fast-growing plant that reaches 18 inches tall. This selection has gray-green foliage.

Gold Cone Juniper (*Juniperus communis* 'Gold Cone'): Upright-growing juniper with bright-yellow foliage.

Chinese Juniper (*Juniperus chinensis* 'Foemina'): Dwarf Chinese juniper used extensively for bonsai. The plant has green leaves and if pruned, the bark takes on an aged look. Usually trained to grow upright.

Dwarf myrtle (*Myrtus communis* 'Compacta'): Compact, dense miniature evergreen shrub that grows slowly. Plant has aromatic foliage and creamy-white flowers in spring.

Dwarf pomegranate (*Punica granatum* 'Nana'): This dwarf pomegranate features dense, medium green foliage and orange-red flowers in the summer. It is deciduous.

Serissa japonica: This bonsai shrub is fine-textured and has deep green foliage and starry white flowers in spring and summer.

Sophora prostrata '**Little Baby**': Very slow-growing tree with eye-catching zigzagged stems and tiny leaves. Often used for bonsai.

Japanese yew (*Taxus Cuspidata* 'Aurea Low Boy'): This low-growing Japanese yew has eye-catching golden-yellow foliage.

Thuja occidentalis '**Danica**': A dwarf evergreen with emerald-green leaves.

Low-growing Groundcovers (Shade)

Baby's Tears (*Soleirolia soleirolii*): Lush, spreading groundcover with dainty green foliage. Plant becomes covered in small white flowers in the summer.

Corsican Mint (*Mentha requienii*): Mat-forming, half-inch high aromatic herb with small, bright green foliage that gives a mossy appearance. Delicate purple flowers cover the plant in the summer.

Dymondia: Ground-hugging plant with 1- to 2-inch-long narrow, gray-green leaves. The plant's leaf margins role up, exposing white undersides. Plant features small, daisy-like yellow flowers in summer.

Golden Stonecrop (*Sedum acre* 'Aureum'): Creeping groundcover with tiny light green succulent leaves. Stem tips turn yellow in spring, and golden, starry flowers cover the plant in summer.

Golden Japanese Stonecrop (*Sedum makinoi* 'Ogon'): Succulent with golden-yellow foliage with pink overtones. The mat-forming plant grows just 2 inches tall. The plant is covered in yellow insignificant flowers in summer.

Midsize Shrubs (Shade)

Adriatic Bellflower (*Campanula garganica* 'Dickson's Gold'): Low-growing, clumping perennial with heart-shaped, lime-green leaves and star-shaped blue flowers in summer.

Cyclamen-miniature: The miniature version of this perennial tuber features 3- to 4-inch-tall plants sporting flowers in pink, white, and red.

Dwarf Hinoki Cypress (*Chamaecyparis obtusa* 'Leprechaun'): Slow-growing dwarf conifer with bright green foliage and a mounding growth habit.

Golden Dwarf Hinoki Cypress (*Chamaecyparis obtusa* 'Nana Lutea'): Small, slow-growing dwarf evergreen plant with lemon-gold foliage.

Variegated Hinoki Cypress (*Chamaecyparis obtusa* 'Cream Tart'): Slow-growing plant with dark green and cream-colored variegated foliage. Grows about 1 inch per year.

Elf Hinoki Cypress (*Chamaecyparis obtusa* 'Elf'): Miniature plant with a dense, semi-conical shape. Plant features tight, dark green foliage.

Hage Hinoki Cypress (*Chamaecyparis obtusa* 'Hage'): Small cypress with a spherical shape. Plant has medium to dark green foliage.

Gold Dust Cypress (*Chamaecyparis pisifera* 'Gold Dust'): Sawara cypress with deep green and yellow variegated foliage. The plant features a mounded growth habit and grows 1 inch a year.

Tsukomo Japanese False Cypress (*Chamaecyparis pisifera* 'Tsukumo'): An extremely slow-growing Sawara cypress with a pyramidal growth pattern. The plant's fine-textured green needles have a blue tinge on the undersides.

Golden Pin Cushion Japanese False Cypress (*Chamaecyparis pisifera* 'Golden Pin Cushion'): Dense dwarf evergreen shrub with golden-green needled foliage.

Silver Lode False Cypress (*Chamaecyparis pisifera* 'Silver Lode'): Variegated false Sawara cypress with green, white, and silver foliage.

White Pigmy False Cypress (*Chamaecyparis pisifera* 'White Pygmy'): Fine-textured false cypress with variegated leaves that feature creamy-white new growth that turns to gray-green.

Hypoestes **'Pink Splash'**: Also known as the pink polka-dot plant, this brightly colored selection features pink foliage veined in green. This perennial plant is generally grown as an annual, but maintains its perennial status in warm climates that experience little to no frost.

Vermont Gold Norway Spruce (*Picea abies* 'Vermont Gold'): Dwarf conifer with whorled lemon-yellow foliage.

Little Gem Norway Spruce (*Picea abies* 'Little Gem'): A dwarf spruce that grows 1 to 2 inches per year. Plant has tiny, dark green needles.

Dans Dwarf Norway Spruce (*Picea abies* 'Dans Dwarf'): Low-growing, mounding spruce with small, light green foliage. Plant grows an inch a year.

Tall "Trees" (Shade)

Variegated English Boxwood (*Buxus sempervirens* 'Aureovariegata'): Slow-growing boxwood with variegated green leaves edged with yellow-gold. Plant has mounded growth habit.

Blue Ball Himalayan Cedar (*Cedrus deodara* 'Blue Ball'): Globe-forming dwarf shrub with blue-green foliage.

Meth's Dwarf White Cedar (*Chamaecyparis Thyoides* 'Meth's Dwarf'): Dwarf white cedar with a conical shape. Gray-green foliage most of the year with a tinge of purple in the winter months.

Top Point White Cedar (*Chamaecyparis Thyoides* 'Top Point'): Cone-shaped small white cedar with blue, soft foliage.

White Cedar (*Chamaecyparis Thyoides* 'Ericoides'): Conifer with a conical, compact growth habit and dense branching. Soft needle-like foliage is blue-green in summer and a red-brown to red-purple in the winter months.

Tansu Japanese Cedar (*Cryptomeria japonica* 'Tansu'): Japanese cedar with fine-textured dark green foliage and an irregular growth habit.

Tenzan Japanese Cedar (*Cryptomeria japonica* 'Tenzan'): Japanese cedar with dense green foliage tinged with orange.

Joel Spingarn Hinoki False Cypress (*Chamaecyparis obtusa* 'Joel Spingarn'): Slow-growing conifer with thick, dark green foliage.

Lawson's Cypress (*Chamaecyparis lawsoniana* 'Green Globe'): Slow-growing miniature shrub with gray-green foliage sometimes splashed with white.

Little Markey Hinoki False Cypress (*Chamaecyparis obtusa* 'Little Markey'): Dwarf evergreen shrub with a mounded form. The foliage is a golden-green.

Lemon Twist Hinoki False Cypress (*Chamaecyparis obtusa* 'Lemon Twist'): Dense, low-growing evergreen shrub with gold and green variegated foliage.

Golden Dwarf Hinoki False Cypress (*Chamaecyparis obtusa* 'Nana Lutea'): A slow-growing dwarf conifer featuring golden-green foliage with yellow highlights.

Twisted Hinoki False Cypress (*Chamaecyparis obtusa* 'Torulosa'): This slow-growing conifer features extremely dense, deep green foliage.

Nana Gracilis Hinoki False Cypress (*Chamaecyparis obtusa* 'Nana Gracilis'): Plant features a pyramidal shape and flattened, drooping branches. The plant's dark green leaves have white markings.

Dainty Doll Hinoki False Cypress (*Chamaecyparis obtusa* 'Dainty Doll'): Slow-growing conifer with finely textured, blue-green foliage. Plant creates a pyramidal shape as it ages.

Verdoni Hinoki False Cypress (*Chamaecyparis obtusa* 'Verdoni'): Dwarf conifer with dark green leaves with gold tips. Plant grows in a loose, pyramidal shape.

Koster's False Cypress (*Chamaecyparis obtusa* 'Kosteri'): Dwarf conifer featuring bright green, twisted foliage.

Dwarf Swara Cypress (*Chamaecyparis pisifera* 'Plumosa Compressa Aurea'): A rounded dwarf cypress with feathery, yellow foliage. Plant is a dense, compact grower.

Treasure Island False Cypress (*Chamaecyparis lawsoniana* 'Treasure'): Slow-growing dwarf conifer with foliage that emerges as yellow in spring and turns golden. The plant's bark is a striking red color.

Red Star False Cypress (*Chamaecyparis thyoides* 'Red Star'): Dwarf soft-textured conifer with blue-green needles that develop an eye-catching red tinge in winter. Plant creates a dense cone shape.

Barry's Silver False Cypress (*Chamaecyparis lawsoniana* 'Barry's Silver'): Slow-growing evergreen with a silvery sheen. Plant has an upright, vase-shaped growth habit.

Blue Gem False Cypress (*Chamaecyparis lawsoniana* 'Blue Gem'): Evergreen with an upright growth habit and blue-green foliage.

Ellwood's Nymph False Cypress (*Chamaecyparis lawsoniana* 'Ellwood's Nymph'): Dwarf tree with a pyramidal shape and dense, soft, blue-green foliage.

Ellwood's Pillar False Cypress (*Chamaecyparis lawsoniana* 'Ellwood's Pillar'): Dwarf narrow, cone-shaped conifer with blue-gray foliage. Dense, compact plant that grows only 3 inches per year.

Silver Threads False Cypress (*Chamaecyparis lawsoniana* 'Silver Threads'): Slow-growing columnar conifer with variegated yellow-green foliage marked by silver-white.

Snow White False Cypress (*Chamaecyparis lawsoniana* 'Snow White'): Teardrop-shaped evergreen with needle-like foliage that is white and matures to blue-green.

Springtime False Cypress (*Chamaecyparis lawsoniana* 'Springtime,'): Dwarf cone-shaped conifer with pale green and golden-yellow foliage.

Treasure Island False Cypress (*Chamaecyparis lawsoniana* 'Treasure'): Slow-growing dwarf conifer with foliage that emerges as yellow in spring and turns golden. The plant's bark is a striking red color.

Blue Surprise False Cypress (*Chamaecyparis lawsoniana* 'Blue Surprise'): Upright-growing conifer with soft, steel-blue foliage.

Ellwood's Gold Pillar False Cypress (*Chamaecyparis lawsoniana* 'Ellwood's Gold Pillar'): Dwarf evergreen pillar-shaped conifer with fluffy, yellow foliage.

Thyme-Leaved Fuchsia (*F. thymifolia*): Low-growing, erect evergreen shrub with delicate, dark-pink fuchsia flowers in summer.

Gentsch Dwarf Globe Hemlock (*Tsuga canadensis* 'Gentsch Dwarf Globe'): Dwarf spherical-shaped plant with soft, green foliage. Plant grows small cones.

Dwarf Japanese Garden Juniper (*Juniper procumbens* 'Nana'): This common bonsai selection is a slow-grower perfect for container growing. The plant's new growth is green, turning to a bluish-green.

Serissa Japonica: This bonsai shrub is fine-textured and has deep green foliage and starry white flowers in spring and summer.

Pixie Dust Alberta Spruce (*Picea glauca* 'Pixie'): Dwarf conical-shaped evergreen with dark-green needled foliage.

Gnome Alberta Spruce (*Picea glauca* 'Gnome'): Mini, slow-growing conifer with an upright cone shape and short green needles.

Little Gem Norway Spruce (*Picea abies* 'Little Gem'): A dwarf spruce that grows 1 to 2 inches per year. Plant has tiny, dark green needles.

***Thuja orientalis* 'Morgan'**: Narrow, columnar dwarf conifer that changes color. In summer, the foliage is lime green, turning to a dark purple in fall and followed by a deep orange in winter.

Irish Yew (*Taxus baccata* 'Fastigiata'): Slow-growing conifer with dark green leaves and an upright, pyramidal shape. Female cultivars produce red berries in fall.

Chapter 9

Decorate for the Holidays!

As discussed in Chapter 3, the addition of a few themed items can transform an existing fairy garden into a charming seasonal scene. For some of us, though, that simply isn't enough! If you find yourself wandering the store aisles for new decorations every holiday and then returning for additional storage bins when the season is over, welcome to the club. Decorating the home and garden for each calendar event keeps the childhood joy of celebration alive.

If every Halloween finds you squeezing in one more jack-o'-lantern or skeleton, or Christmas demands that you add another string of lights and a new box of ornaments to the tree, or, for that matter, another completely decorated tree—then it's official. Like so many of us, you are a holiday fanatic!

Creating a fairy garden for one specific occasion is a natural extension of using seasonal themes throughout the house. After all, the porch or walkway often finds wreaths, pumpkins, bunnies, and flags announcing each holiday to guests arriving at the front door. Why not include a mini landscape filled with items that make each celebration meaningful to your family and friends?

When planning your garden, decide if you want a representation of the general season or a true portrayal of each holiday. If you choose the latter, it will only be showcased for four to six weeks before it's time to redecorate. A very generic planting can be used as a backdrop for various scenes; for instance, a "tree" toward the back of the pot with one midsize "shrub" in the middle and a low-growing groundcover in the front. But to really advance into a fantasy creation, fresh plantings for each scene will be needed. Bear in mind that you can reuse the plants in another configuration. A garden that is only a couple of months old can easily be "torn apart" and the various plants can either be used in the next garden or put into smaller pots to save them for a future scene. (Keep the plants well watered for a few days after transplanting and then just water normally.)

For many, October is the start of the major holiday season. Cool nights and crisp mornings mean Halloween is just around the corner. The scenario pictured on the previous page has all of the classic elements of a haunted house—from the tombstones and pumpkins, to the eerie gate featuring pillars. The planting is kept simple and could easily be used for another seasonal look. Spanish moss draped around the basket provides a spooky feel but can be quickly removed after the holiday passes.

Recycling old décor can be the beginning of a charming (outdoor) tabletop garden. This homage to Thanksgiving was inspired by a long-neglected cornucopia. Think of what each holiday personifies and choose accessories that reflect that theme. The abundance of a harvest is represented here by the table full of goodies and miniature basket filled to the brim with nature's bounty.

Reuse, repurpose! Who hasn't been given one of the huge tins of popcorn that seem to be in every store during Christmas? Punch some holes in the bottom, fill it halfway up with some packing peanuts (to lessen the weight if you want to move it around), and then continue filling it with potting soil. This gives you the perfect home for a cozy Christmas setting. Bring it inside for a few hours during the big family party, but remember to put it back outdoors immediately afterward.

Mini-tip: Stringing Popcorn

Most packaging Styrofoam is made of compressed "beads." Gently separate the packaging into the little spherical pieces and string with a needle and thread to make a waterproof strand of "popcorn" for trees.

Since each holiday has its own theme, your choices will determine how you want to interpret these special days. Let those first thoughts that pop into your consciousness be your guide. What images does Valentine's Day conjure? Hearts are usually the quintessential symbol of the day and a bold sprinkling of them throughout the garden leaves no doubt to the viewer which red-letter day you're celebrating!

A tisket a tasket, remodel that old basket! If the Easter bunny wants to bring a brand-new container for the eggs this year, grab the old one and start a spring-filled garden in it. Line the basket with sphagnum moss before adding your soil and look for a few blooming plants to suggest a view filled with flowers. This scene boasts a white serissa and pink cuphea "tree," along with some pink erodium in the foreground. The white-flowered erigeron behind the baby fairy and variegated erodium behind her big sister complete the illusion of an English garden in full bloom. A teensy basket filled with "dyed" eggs (made from craft clay) is a marvelous juxtaposition with the life-size model in which the garden is planted. Scattering

more eggs throughout the tableau suggests the action of an Easter egg hunt still in progress. Adding a few sweet rabbits to the depiction keeps that "Fairy Focus" magic working.

Fly the flag proudly and let her colors serve as the palette for a Fourth of July extravaganza. Notice how everything in the fairy garden on the prior page relates to the red, white, and blue—from the fairies themselves to the table, wagon, container, and even the animals. The barbecue in the backdrop, pies on the picnic table, and soft drinks icing in the tin tub are a slice of Americana activity of which Yankee Doodle himself would approve.

If space is limited and building a garden for one particular holiday isn't practical, consider devoting a spot to a seasonal display. Changing it out four times a year will still give you ample opportunities to delight guests with depictions of nature's constant changes. Making this type of garden is a terrific excuse to treasure hunt at the nearest thrift store for containers that will inspire you to look beyond the norm.

This celebration of spring started with a wood carry-all. Brightly hued flowers were used rather than the usual miniature plantings, but the all-important aspect of telling a story is still intact. This time, the fairies are interacting with the human-size accessories—sitting on the trowel, tiptoeing across the handle, and tugging on the thumb of the glove. This would be fantastic not only in the welcoming setting of your home, but as a centerpiece for a springtime event or garden wedding. Using inexpensive annuals is also cost-effective for when you need to provide multiple table decorations. (Just reuse the fairies in your own mini creations later.)

The lazy days of summer just call out for a picnic. This basket is a secondhand shop find and is an economical way to present the sun-filled season. Mini plants combined with full-size items bring the everyday world and Fairyland together into a charming mix. The repurposed plates, glasses, and picnic basket cost only a few dollars and after several cheery toasts emptied it, the bottle was free!

The earthy tones of fall are reflected in this autumn scene. The pumpkin house is cradled by the warm-colored foliage of the tree, and the rusty fence matches the scrolled planter that anchors the garden. The fairy crossing to meet her friendly froggy neighbor was originally used in the springtime scene.

Winter, when so much of nature takes a nap, provides a beautiful panorama for our final garden of the season. For those of us living in mild climates, "dreaming of a white Christmas" is just that—a childlike fantasy of the world in subtle shades of blues and whites. When selecting your plants, search for ones that stay in that color range, as doing so imparts an ethereal quality to the overall look. White rock gives the idea of a snowy coating and using a mirror (remember to spray the back to protect it) for a small frozen pond reflects not only the fairy and bunnies, but the tiny battery-operated twinkle lights in the tree. White accessories are a natural match to the landscape and make this scene a lovely way to end a wonderful year.

Resources

A wide variety of accessory and plant resources exist for fairy gardening. Here is a sampling:

Echo Valley

www.echovalley.com

800-592-9678

P.O. Box 2741

Ann Arbor, MI 48106

Carry a selection of fairy garden accessories, climbing gnomes, gazebos and garden gates, carts, wishing wells, urn planters, reflection pools, and wishing wells. Also feature solar fairies to illuminate the garden.

Efairies.com

www.efairies.com

360-455-0334

502 Custer Way SE, Suite A

Tumwater, WA 98501

Selection of fairies and gnomes, including fountains, houses, miniature furniture, solar and fairy lights, stepping stones, green rubber boots, hanging baskets, and miniature plants and flowers. Also offer gothic, zodiac, and pewter fairies.

Enchanted Gardens

www.miniature-gardens.com

888-642-5122

Carry a wide selection of fairy accessories, including fairies and gnomes, animal figurines, cottages, wrought-iron arbors and gazebos, wood and metal bridges, bird baths, wooden boats, wishing wells, twig tables and chairs, metal bicycles, furniture, tools, fencing, miniature dishware, and Christmas miniatures.

Fairy Gardens

www.fairygardens.com

5920-200th St. SW #42

Lynnwood, WA 98036

Sell fairy figurines, fairy furniture sets, tin hand tools, resin gardening hats, gloves, watering cans, and shoes. Also feature garden swings and trellises, wheelbarrows, and Adirondack rockers.

Fairy Garden Expert

www.fairygardenexpert.net

714-538-8042

M & M Nursery

380 North Tustin St.

Orange, CA 92867

Offer a complete line of high-quality fairies and animal figurines, as well as accessories. Carry fairy houses, arbors, gazebos, miniature garden pots, fairy furniture, birdbaths, gazing balls, tea party sets, wedding cakes, wheelbarrows, teensy statuary, holiday and seasonal accents, and specialty miniature fairy plants.

Fairy Homes and Gardens

www.fairyhomesandgardens.com

816-294-8972

1106 South Hwy 71

Savannah, MO 64485

Offer fairies and gnomes, churches, ceramic and living-roof cottages, toad houses, arbors, trellises, gates, birdbaths, fairy pets, and doors. Also available are plant packages of miniature full-sun perennials.

Georgetown Home and Garden

http://georgetownusa.com

877-213-6279

22135 68th Ave. S.

Kent, WA 98032

Feature an array of fine-quality fairy accessories from their Fiddlehead fairy™ collection, including statues, fairy village houses, gnomes, twig garden benches, chairs, bistro sets, cement and metal birdbaths, and gazing balls. Additional items include a miniature patio mix kit, small ponds that you can add real water to, a fairy cave, and small bottles of pixie dust.

Homespun Treasures

www.homespunwalnutcreek.com

330-893-2134

3147 Ohio 39

Millersburg, OH 44654

A wide range of garden accessories, including stepping stones, wishing benches, checkerboard bistro sets, leafed chairs, birdbaths, gazing balls, mini bricks, and vine fences. Also offer pots, lanterns, nests, garden edgings, mini Adirondack chairs, and picnic tables.

Market Hill-Fine Fairy Houses

www.finefairyhouses.com

877-224-5650

11905 Market Ave.

Cologne MN 55322

Sell various ceramic gnome-style fairy houses and accessories, including chandeliers, gazebos, bridges, mailboxes, insects, lawnmowers, birdhouses, trellises, and furniture. Also offer value-priced accessory and fairy garden kits.

Miniature Cottage

www.miniaturecottage.com

615-298-2872

410 East Iris Dr.

Nashville, TN 37204

Feature stone planters, antique garden furniture, bridges, arbors, columns, urns, parterre's gates, staircases, and benches. Special items include glass cloches, bicycles, teatime armchairs, watering cans, rabbits, and gnomes.

Natural Havens

http://naturalhavens.net

608-228-0400

Sell a wide selection of specialty fairy items, including fairy figurines, fairy houses, benches, tables, twig chairs, arbors, bridges, fences, birdbaths, gazing balls, birdfeeders, lanterns, and buckets. Also featured are defining structures, fire-pit groupings, copper obelisks, swings, metal willow arbors, fences, bridges, stepping stones, and patio pads.

Obsession With Butterflies

http://obsessionwithbutterflies.com

Enchanting range of elves, flower and herb fairies, as well as arches, gates, and fences. Also carry butterfly houses and larvae.

Plow & Hearth

www.plowhearth.com

800-494-7544

Offer planters, woodland furniture, elf doors and windows, gnomes, and gnome homes. Products also include resin and metal fairy garden accessories, and fairy village pieces.

Summers Past Farms

http://summerspastfarms.com

15602 Olde Highway 80

Flinn Springs, CA 92021

619-390-1523

Carry hand-painted signs, watering cans, garden tools, arbors, gates, birdbaths, fairy picks, garden paths, figurines, and cottages. Also have various designed garden kits and complete deluxe adornments for creating garden scenes.

The Enchanted World of Fairy Woodland

http://www.fairywoodland.com

800-304-3795

P.O. Box 868

Newport, OR 97365

Offer fairy houses and habitats, furniture, bases and stands, ponds, wishing wells, woodsy doors and windows, dining sets, tea tables, and branch chairs. In addition, sell forest sprites and fairy theaters playhouses.

The Fairy's Garden

www.thefairysgarden.com

877-929-9282

5310 East Main St.

Maple Plain, MN 55359

Offer an interesting selection of garden dwellings, outbuildings, bridges, walls, gateways, and enclosures. Additional items include well-priced garden adornments, birdbaths, pixie posts, urns, garden seats, and woodland creatures.

The Pure Gardener

www.thepuregardener.com

630-232-2766

502 W. State St.

Geneva, IL 60134

Sell fairies, galvanized zinc mushrooms, bee skeps, birdhouses and birdbath picks, leaf fire pit sets, and chandeliers. In addition, offer miniature bird nests and eggs, garden parterres, and edging.

Wee Trees

www.weetrees.com

419-410-9534

3131 Wilkins Rd.

Swanton, OH 43558

Carry fairies, gnomes, dogs, flamingos, turtles and frogs, gazebos, arbors, doors, garden furniture, and wee buildings. Also offer mini gardens sets, including greenery, trees, shrubs, vines, ground covers, and grasses.

Acknowledgments

The authors would like to thank Jill Marsal of Marsal Lyon Literary Agency for her belief in the book and dedication to seeing it in print. We are also deeply grateful to Ted Mayeda for his assistance, encouragement, and the use of M & M Nursery as the home of the original fairy garden. A big thank-you goes to Xuong Do of Happy Photos for his truly magical photos of the fairy gardens you see in this book. Thanks also to Jeremy Davis, who helped design a successful proposal, Sabrina Davis for her trained eye and keen insights, and Danny Davis for always being available to do the heavy lifting. Final words of appreciation go to garden columnist Cindy McNatt for encouraging the collaboration and to journalist Jerry Rice for reviewing the project in the proposal stage.

About the Authors

JULIE BAWDEN-DAVIS

Julie Bawden-Davis began developing her green thumb about the same time she started writing. As a child, she filled her home with houseplants and diligently took notes on their progress and growth habits.

Since graduating from California State University, Long Beach, in 1985 with a bachelor's in journalism, Bawden-Davis has gathered a vast array of garden writing credentials. She is author of several books, including *Indoor Gardening the Organic Way: How to Create a Natural and Sustaining Environment for Your Houseplants* (2007), *Reader's Digest Flower Gardening* (2004/2012), *Houseplants & Indoor Gardening: Decorating Your Home with Houseplants* (2002), and *The Strawberry Story: How to Grow Great Berries in Southern California* (1993/2013). She regularly lectures on gardening and does book signings throughout Southern California.

Bawden-Davis has written well over 1,500 articles for a wide variety of publications, including *Better Homes & Gardens*, *Organic Gardening*, *Wildflower Magazine*, HGTV.com, *Family Circle*, *Parents*, *The Los Angeles Times*, and *The San Francisco Chronicle*. She is also founder of HealthyHouseplants.com, a plant care expert for TheMulch.com, and co-owner of Exotic

Edibles & Ornamentals, which she runs with her sister, Amy Bawden.

A member of the Garden Writer's Association (GWA) and the American Society of Journalists and Authors (ASJA), Bawden-Davis was also certified in 1998 as a University of California Master Gardener. She lives, writes, and gardens indoors and out in Southern California.

BEVERLY TURNER

Beverly Turner is one of the leading authorities on miniature fairy gardening. Her creations have inspired a devotion to the tiny landscapes among the thousands who have attended her sold-out seminars. In addition to twenty years in the nursery industry, Turner is an accomplished actress, director, and set designer, whose work has appeared in more than 100 productions throughout California.

She was part of an improvisational comedy group, Nobody's Fools, for two years, toured with Renegadi, a Commedia dell'Arte troupe, and was a featured performer at the original Renaissance Pleasure Faire in Agoura, California, for four seasons. Six years as a founding member of the Shakespeare Company Bard in the Yard was followed by two decades spent acting and directing at various local theaters.

A fortuitous search for part-time work twenty years ago led to the two great loves of her life—her husband and soulmate, Allan, and gardening! While employed at her husband's nursery, Turner found that her skills as a theatrical designer led to a fresh approach to garden displays. Her ability to take seemingly unrelated objects and plant material and mesh them into something unique has been imitated by customers for years.

It is Turner's ability to view the world with a designer's eye that initially led her to create fairy gardens over a decade ago. While working on an always-longed-for dollhouse, she discovered that the real attraction wasn't the house itself, but the wee flowers and accessories she made. Friends and family admired the scaled-down perfection and wished it could be re-created using live plants. Turner rose to the challenge and began researching the availability and practicality of growing fairy-size trees and flowers in containers. Her resulting miniature gardens are a constant source of admiration. Some devotees have literally crossed the country to tap into her expertise. She lives, acts, and gardens in Southern California.

Index

THE
APACHE

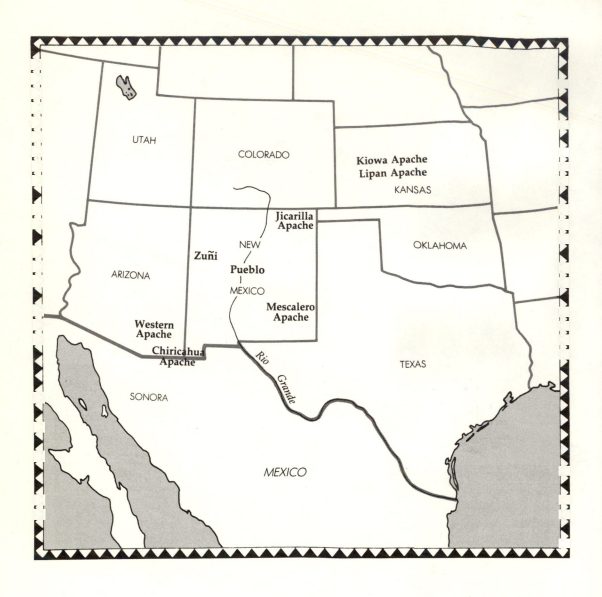

UTAH

COLORADO

Kiowa Apache
Lipan Apache

KANSAS

Jicarilla
Apache

NEW

Zuñi

OKLAHOMA

Pueblo

ARIZONA

MEXICO

Mescalero
Apache

Western
Apache

Chiricahua
Apache

TEXAS

Rio Grande

SONORA

MEXICO

THE
APACHE

Michael E. Melody
Barry University

Frank W. Porter III
General Editor

CHELSEA HOUSE PUBLISHERS
New York   Philadelphia

On the cover Headdress worn by an Apache masked dancer

Chelsea House Publishers
Editor-in-Chief Nancy Toff
Executive Editor Remmel T. Nunn
Managing Editor Karyn Gullen Browne
Copy Chief Juliann Barbato
Picture Editor Adrian G. Allen
Art Director Maria Epes
Manufacturing Manager Gerald Levine

Indians of North America
Senior Editor Sam Tanenhaus

Staff for **THE APACHE**
Deputy Copy Chief Ellen Scordato
Editorial Assistant Tara P. Deal
Assistant Art Director Laurie Jewell
Designer Victoria Tomaselli
Picture Researcher Nisa Rauschenberg
Production Coordinator Joseph Romano

First Printing

1 3 5 7 9 8 6 4 2

Library of Congress Cataloging in Publication Data

Melody, Michael Edward.
The Apache

(Indians of North America)
Bibliography: p.
Includes index.
1. Apache Indians—Bibliography. I. Porter, Frank W.,
1947– . II. Title. III. Series: Indians of North America
(Chelsea House Publishers)
Z1210.A6M43   1988   016.97'000497   88-9587
[E99.A6]
ISBN 1-55546-689-3
        0-7910-0352-3 (pbk.)

CONTENTS

INDIANS OF NORTH AMERICA

The Abenaki

American Indian
  Literature

The Apache

The Arapaho

The Archaeology
  of North America

The Aztecs

The Cahuilla

The Catawba

The Cherokee

The Cheyenne

The Chickasaw

The Chinook

The Chipewyan

The Choctaw

The Chumash

The Coast Salish
  Peoples

The Comanche

The Creek

The Crow

The Eskimo

Federal Indian Policy

The Hidatsa

The Huron

The Iroquois

The Kiowa

The Kwakiutl

The Lenape

The Lumbee

The Maya

The Menominee

The Modoc

The Montagnais-Naskapi

The Nanticoke

The Narragansett

The Navajo

The Nez Perce

The Ojibwa

The Osage

The Paiute

The Pima-Maricopa

The Potawatomi

The Powhatan Tribes

The Pueblo

The Quapaw

The Seminole

The Tarahumara

The Tunica-Biloxi

Urban Indians

The Wampanoag

Women in American
  Indian Society

The Yakima

The Yankton Sioux

The Yuma

CHELSEA HOUSE PUBLISHERS

INDIANS OF NORTH AMERICA: CONFLICT AND SURVIVAL

Frank W. Porter III

*The Indians survived our
open intention of wiping them
out, and since the tide turned
they have even weathered
our good intentions toward them,
which can be much more deadly.*

John Steinbeck
America and Americans

When Europeans first reached the North American continent, they found hundreds of tribes occupying a vast and rich country. The newcomers quickly recognized the wealth of natural resources. They were not, however, so quick or willing to recognize the spiritual, cultural, and intellectual riches of the people they called Indians.

The Indians of North America examines the problems that develop when people with different cultures come together. For American Indians, the consequences of their interaction with non-Indian people have been both productive and tragic. The Europeans believed they had "discovered" a "New World," but their religious bigotry, cultural bias, and materialistic world view kept them from appreciating and understanding the people who lived in it. All too often they attempted to change the way of life of the indigenous people. The Spanish conquistadores wanted the Indians as a source of labor. The Christian missionaries, many of whom were English, viewed them as potential converts. French traders and trappers used the Indians as a means to obtain pelts. As Francis Parkman, the 19th-century historian, stated, "Spanish civilization crushed the Indian; English civilization scorned and neglected him; French civilization embraced and cherished him."

Nearly 500 years later, many people think of American Indians as curious vestiges of a distant past, waging a futile war to survive in a Space Age society. Even today, our understanding of the history and culture of American Indians is too often derived from unsympathetic, culturally biased, and inaccurate reports. The American Indian, described and portrayed in thousands of movies, television programs, books, articles, and government studies, has either been raised to the status of the "noble savage" or disparaged as the "wild Indian" who resisted the westward expansion of the American frontier.

Where in this popular view are the real Indians, the human beings and communities whose ancestors can be traced back to ice-age hunters? Where are the creative and indomitable people whose sophisticated technologies used the natural resources to ensure their survival, whose military skill might even have prevented European settlement of North America if not for devastating epidemics and the disruption of the ecology? Where are the men and women who are today diligently struggling to assert their legal rights and express once again the value of their heritage?

The various Indian tribes of North America, like people everywhere, have a history that includes population expansion, adaptation to a range of regional environments, trade across wide networks, internal strife, and warfare. This was the reality. Europeans justified their conquests, however, by creating a mythical image of the New World and its native people. In this myth, the New World was a virgin land, waiting for the Europeans. The arrival of Christopher Columbus ended a timeless primitiveness for the original inhabitants.

Also part of this myth was the debate over the origins of the American Indians. Fantastic and diverse answers were proposed by the early explorers, missionaries, and settlers. Some thought that the Indians were descended from the Ten Lost Tribes of Israel, others that they were descended from inhabitants of the lost continent of Atlantis. One writer suggested that the Indians had reached North America in another Noah's ark.

A later myth, perpetrated by many historians, focused on the relentless persecution during the past five centuries until only a scattering of these "primitive" people remained to be herded onto reservations. This view fails to chronicle the overt and covert ways in which the Indians successfully coped with the intruders.

All of these myths presented one-sided interpretations that ignored the complexity of European and American events and policies. All left serious questions unanswered. What were the origins of the American Indians? Where did they come from? How and when did they get to the New World? What was their life—their culture—really like?

In the late 1800s, anthropologists and archaeologists in the Smithsonian Institution's newly created Bureau of American Ethnology in Washington, D. C., began to study scientifically the history and culture of the Indians of North America. They were motivated by an honest belief that the Indians were on the verge of extinction and that along with them would vanish their languages, religious beliefs, technology, myths, and legends. These men and women went out to visit, study, and record data from as many Indian communities as possible before this information was forever lost.

8

By this time there was a new myth in the national consciousness. American Indians existed as figures in the American past. They had performed a historical mission. They had challenged white settlers who trekked across the continent. Once conquered, however, they were supposed to accept graciously the way of life of their conquerors.

The reality again was different. American Indians resisted both actively and passively. They refused to lose their unique identity, to be assimilated into white society. Many whites viewed the Indians not only as members of a conquered nation but also as "inferior" and "unequal." The rights of the Indians could be expanded, contracted, or modified as the conquerors saw fit. In every generation, white society asked itself what to do with the American Indians. Their answers have resulted in the twists and turns of federal Indian policy.

There were two general approaches. One way was to raise the Indians to a "higher level" by "civilizing" them. Zealous missionaries considered it their Christian duty to elevate the Indian through conversion and scanty education. The other approach was to ignore the Indians until they disappeared under pressure from the ever-expanding white society. The myth of the "vanishing Indian" gave stronger support to the latter option, helping to justify the taking of the Indians' land.

Prior to the end of the 18th century, there was no national policy on Indians simply because the American nation had not yet come into existence. American Indians similarly did not possess a political or social unity with which to confront the various Europeans. They were not homogeneous. Rather, they were loosely formed bands and tribes, speaking nearly 300 languages and thousands of dialects. The collective identity felt by Indians today is a result of their common experiences of defeat and/or mistreatment at the hands of whites.

During the colonial period, the British crown did not have a coordinated policy toward the Indians of North America. Specific tribes (most notably the Iroquois and the Cherokee) became military and political pawns used by both the crown and the individual colonies. The success of the American Revolution brought no immediate change. When the United States acquired new territory from France and Mexico in the early 19th century, the federal government wanted to open this land to settlement by homesteaders. But the Indian tribes that lived on this land had signed treaties with European governments assuring their title to the land. Now the United States assumed legal responsibility for honoring these treaties.

At first, President Thomas Jefferson believed that the Louisiana Purchase contained sufficient land for both the Indians and the white population.

Within a generation, though, it became clear that the Indians would not be allowed to remain. In the 1830s the federal government began to coerce the eastern tribes to sign treaties agreeing to relinquish their ancestral land and move west of the Mississippi River. Whenever these negotiations failed, President Andrew Jackson used the military to remove the Indians. The southeastern tribes, promised food and transportation during their removal to the West, were instead forced to walk the "Trail of Tears." More than 4,000 men, women, and children died during this forced march. The "removal policy" was successful in opening the land to homesteaders, but it created enormous hardships for the Indians.

By 1871 most of the tribes in the United States had signed treaties ceding most or all of their ancestral land in exchange for reservations and welfare. The treaty terms were intended to bind both parties for all time. But in the General Allotment Act of 1887, the federal government changed its policy again. Now the goal was to make tribal members into individual landowners and farmers, encouraging their absorption into white society. This policy was advantageous to whites who were eager to acquire Indian land, but it proved disastrous for the Indians. One hundred thirty-eight million acres of reservation land were subdivided into tracts of 160, 80, or as little as 40 acres, and allotted to tribe members on an individual basis. Land owned in this way was said to have "trust status" and could not be sold. But the surplus land—all Indian land not allotted to individuals— was opened (for sale) to white settlers. Ultimately, more than 90 million acres of land were taken from the Indians by legal and illegal means.

The resulting loss of land was a catastrophe for the Indians. It was necessary to make it illegal for Indians to sell their land to non-Indians. The Indian Reorganization Act of 1934 officially ended the allotment period. Tribes that voted to accept the provisions of this act were reorganized, and an effort was made to purchase land within preexisting reservations to restore an adequate land base.

Ten years later, in 1944, federal Indian policy again shifted. Now the federal government wanted to get out of the "Indian business." In 1953 an act of Congress named specific tribes whose trust status was to be ended "at the earliest possible time." This new law enabled the United States to end unilaterally, whether the Indians wished it or not, the special status that protected the land in Indian tribal reservations. In the 1950s federal Indian policy was to transfer federal responsibility and jurisdiction to state governments, encourage the physical relocation of Indian peoples from reservations to urban areas, and hasten the termination, or extinction, of tribes.

Between 1954 and 1962 Congress passed specific laws authorizing the termination of more than 100 tribal groups. The stated purpose of the termination policy was to ensure the full and complete integration of Indians into American society. However, there is a less benign way to interpret this legislation. Even as termination was being discussed in Congress, 133 separate bills were introduced to permit the transfer of trust land ownership from Indians to non-Indians.

With the Johnson administration in the 1960s the federal government began to reject termination. In the 1970s yet another Indian policy emerged. Known as "self-determination," it favored keeping the protective role of the federal government while increasing tribal participation in, and control of, important areas of local government. In 1983 President Reagan, in a policy statement on Indian affairs, restated the unique "government to government" relationship of the United States with the Indians. However, federal programs since then have moved toward transferring Indian affairs to individual states, which have long desired to gain control of Indian land and resources.

As long as American Indians retain power, land, and resources that are coveted by the states and the federal government, there will continue to be a "clash of cultures," and the issues will be contested in the courts, Congress, the White House, and even in the international human rights community. To give all Americans a greater comprehension of the issues and conflicts involving American Indians today is a major goal of this series. These issues are not easily understood, nor can these conflicts be readily resolved. The study of North American Indian history and culture is a necessary and important step toward that comprehension. All Americans must learn the history of the relations between the Indians and the federal government, recognize the unique legal status of the Indians, and understand the heritage and cultures of the Indians of North America.

The harsh desert terrain of the American Southwest hardened the Apache into fierce nomads.

THE GAME OF SURVIVAL

Long ago, many creatures—but no humans—populated the earth. Huge beasts stalked the land, and vast serpents slithered across it. These creatures were always famished, so they fed on small birds as well as on wolves, rabbits, and squirrels. The small creatures tried to flee, but because the world was shrouded in eternal darkness they could not see where they were going.

One day all the creatures—large and small—met on Mescal Mountain, which rose above the desert in what is now New Mexico. A debate concerning daylight began. The monsters, beasts, and serpents wanted the world to remain dark so they could continue to pursue the smaller animals, who, of course, favored daylight. After a lengthy quarrel, the two sides agreed to settle the issue with a game. Each side dug many holes in the ground and hid sticks in one of them. The other side then tried to guess which hole held the sticks. If they

guessed correctly they gained possession of the sticks. The side that won all the sticks would be declared the champion and would slaughter the losers.

The contest was close. First the small creatures—led by the birds—forged ahead, collecting several sticks. Then the beasts rallied. Eventually, the birds were left with only a single stick and faced a terrible loss. One hope remained. At the start of the game, a large bird, Turkey, had placed some sticks in his moccasin and wandered off to nap. Now the other birds ran to awaken him. Turkey brought his sticks and joined the game. A deft player, he helped the birds win back many sticks. They even took some held by the beasts and moved into the lead. Soon the beasts were down to only a handful, and, to their amazement, the sky, which had always been pitch black, filled with light. Wren, a small songbird, chirped, "Daybreak is coming! Daybreak is coming!'' The beasts lost their last stick, and the birds started to kill them.

In their excitement the birds set upon one of the most fearsome beasts, Giant. They removed arrows from their quivers and shot at him, but they failed to pierce his heart. Giant still lived. Suddenly, one of the beasts, Lizard, changed sides and came to the aid of the birds. He knew that Giant's heart was lodged in the underside of his foot. He aimed an arrow there, and at last Giant was slain. The other beasts panicked and fled, chased by the birds. They shot arrows at Snake, but he slith-

ered into a crevice on a cliff where they could not reach him. Thus, though no giants inhabit the earth today, the desert is filled with snakes.

This story—which pits large animals in a violent contest against smaller ones and whose outcome seems a matter of sheer luck—provides many clues to the culture from which it originated: that of the Apache. These people inhabited the Great Plains and the deserts of Texas, New Mexico, and Arizona, in what is now called the American Southwest.

This region has a harsh and changeable climate. Fierce winds whip year

The Apache moved seasonally, usually to pursue game. When they set up camp they assembled portable dwellings, made of brush, that could be dismantled and carried to new sites.

Though renowned as warriors, Apache leaders often sought peace with the U.S. Army. An especially peaceful Apache was Eskiminzin (far right), who in the 1870s led a Western Apache band in Arizona.

round over the level acreage. In the summer, they gust up from the south with the intensity of flames. Autumn winds, often from the southeast, bring warmer air. And in the winter, chilly winds funnel down from the north. The Apache weathered these extremes by living as nomads. Their only permanent home was the land itself, which they roamed as the seasons changed and as the animals they hunted—deer, elk, an-

telope, and buffalo—sought out comfortable temperatures and grassy places where they could graze.

As the legend of the birds and the beasts attests, the stark environment of the plains taught the Apache to view life as a contest—fought against the elements and against other humans. The various Apache groups generally stayed on peaceful terms with one another but made no· effort to uphold

In the 20th century, Mescalero Apache replaced war-horses with tractors and farmed the barren soil of their reservation in southern New Mexico.

peaceful relations with other Indians. The Apache engaged in long-running feuds with the Pawnee and other Plains tribes: the Pima, Papago, and the Sobaipuri.

The Apache, perhaps more than most other Indian groups, were warriors. They took up arms for many reasons—in disputes over trading, hunting, and territorial rights; to seek revenge; and in immediate retaliation for recently committed wrongs. Thus, the Apache gained a reputation for being among the most warlike of Native-American groups. Even their name

conveys ferocity. *Apache* derives from *ápachu* and means "enemy"—not in the language used by these people themselves but in the tongue spoken by the Zuni, a sedentary southwestern tribe that traded with them in the 16th century. By 1598, *ápachu* was the term most commonly used by other Indian groups.

By the time white people arrived on their territory in the mid-1500s, the Apache had hardened into talented and fearless warriors prepared to meet any intrusion with force. First, they clashed with Spanish *conquistadores*—or conquerors—who had many advantages over the Apache, including horses and firearms. The Apache developed a taste for both items and often traded for or stole them. The Spaniards did not venture far into Apache territory, but in the 17th, 18th, and 19th centuries the culture they perpetuated in Mexico steadily encroached on Apache lands. In the 1820s, when Mexico shook off its colonial yoke and became an independent republic, its citizens often skirmished with the Apache, who sought to protect their land, their buffalo, and their practice of raiding for food, equipment, and human captives. Then, in the 1840s and 1850s, after Mexico ceded vast territory to the United States, the Apache squared off against a new batch of intruders: American soldiers, gold prospectors, and settlers.

Fierce as the Apache were, their entire population numbered only about 5,000 and did not form a unified nation such as that of the Lakota or the Sioux. Nor did they have tribal leaders. Instead they broke down into much smaller units that lived, hunted, raided, and warred on their own. By the 1860s, most of these bands—which could include up to a hundred warriors—waged protracted battles against the U.S. Army and also against vigilantes, or loosely organized but heavily armed groups of civilians.

Atrocities abounded on both sides, as the Americans sought to subdue the Apache and pin them within the margins of the land they had once roamed freely. Though badly overmatched, the Apache held off the Americans until the late 19th century. Their war leaders—Mangas Coloradas, Cochise, Geronimo, and Victorio—rank among the most renowned Indians in American history.

In the end, the Apache succumbed to the superior numbers and firepower of their adversaries. No Apache band was ever really conquered, but all eventually submitted and accepted the terms dictated by the white man. They laid down their arms, gave up their nomadic way of life, and moved onto reservations—mainly worthless tracts of land set aside by the U.S. government. There they have struggled since to subsist as farmers, ranchers, sheepherders, and businesspeople, while retaining their ancestral language, customs, and beliefs.

Contemporary Apache keep alive the memory of their ancestors, products and custodians of the land who fought fiercely to maintain their independence against overwhelming odds. Their story is one of the tragedies of American history, but it is filled with incidents of triumph and lit throughout with heroism and pride. ▲

Three Apache women pose with samples of their handiwork. The Apache produced some of the finest basketry made by American Indians.

ORIGINS
AND
HABITS

Originally, the Apache belonged to the Athapaskan federation, a people who inhabited the region of the North American continent in and around present-day Alaska and northwestern Canada. No one knows exactly why the Apache left this territory, nor exactly when, but it is certain that between A.D. 1000 and A.D. 1500 this group joined a mass southward migration of Athapaskan who had broken away from the larger group.

Journeying south along the eastern edge of the Rocky Mountains, the Athapaskan proceeded into the western part of the Great Plains—the present-day states of Colorado, New Mexico, and Utah. By the 1400s signs of Apache life appeared in various pockets of a vast territory that covered much of the American Southwest. This region stretched some 800 miles north to south (from Kansas down to northern Mexico) and some 200 to 400 miles east to west

(from Oklahoma to Arizona). It encompassed parts of Texas and Colorado and all of New Mexico.

Because the Apache were nomads, ready on short notice to take all their belongings and move to new campsites, they lived in small groups that were mobile and could easily settle in new places. Each of these groups, formed from a network of blood relatives, staked out its own territory and became self-sufficient.

During wartime, groups merged into larger units—several hundred people strong—called bands. These bands took on the characteristics of tribes, with their own language, customs, and organization. Today the bands are identified by Spanish names given them by the first white people with whom they came into contact.

The bands can be distinguished best by geography. The easternmost Apache group was the Kiowa-Apache, who blended in with the Kiowa nation in modern-day Kansas and Oklahoma. Next came the Lipan, who lived in the lower Rio Grande valley in New Mexico and Mexico and ranged toward the Texas coast. Farther west were the Jicarilla. They lived in northern New Mexico and southern Colorado and camped and hunted along the Rio Grande, near modern-day Santa Fe. The Mescalero inhabited New Mexico, ranged from the Rio Grande in the west to the Pecos River area in southwestern Texas (near the town of Pecos), and hunted and camped in northern Mex-

ico. Farther west, in New Mexico and also in Arizona, lived the Chiricahua. Finally, there were the Western Apache, who comprised five major subgroups—the White Mountain Apache, the San Carlos Apache, the Cibecue Apache, the Southern Tonto, and the Northern Tonto—all of whom resided in east-central Arizona, just above the Mexican border.

Despite these geographical distinctions, the various Apache bands viewed themselves as a single, related people. The Apache called themselves *N'de*, *Dĭnï*, *Tindé*, or *Indé*—all derived from

The Kiowa, Jicarilla, and Chiricahua Apache lived in tipis, cone-shaped dwellings with earthen floors.

the term *tinneh*, meaning "the people" superior to all other humans, whom they regarded as members of an inferior species.

The various Apache groups were linked by their physical appearance. Most Apache men were of medium stature, thin and well muscled, and had enormous stamina. Warriors could run 50 miles without stopping to rest and were so swift they could outdistance mounted troops. This uncanny ability would play a significant role in their encounter with the U.S. Army. Most Apache women, several inches shorter than the men, were slender and lithe.

The dwellings built by the different Apache groups were also similar. The Kiowa, Jicarilla, and some Chiricahua lived in tipis, or cone-shaped dwellings covered with animal hides. Most Apache, however, lived in *wickiups*—circular or oval huts made of brush, with earthen floors scooped out to enlarge the living area. As the seasons changed, so did the wickiup's outer coverings. In summer, leafy branches were draped over the dwelling; in winter, animal hides, expertly tanned, provided insulation. For added warmth, the Apache burned a fire on the earthen floor (if the hut was big enough), and smoke escaped through a small hole in the roof.

In any case, these homes were temporary—suitable for a people whose lives followed the pattern of the seasons. The Chiricahua placed their wickiups close together and burned them in preparation for their winter migration,

Apache wickiups *were circular huts whose coverings could be changed. Animal hides (shown here) provided insulation in the winter; in the summer, brush helped keep the dwellers cool.*

when they traveled far into the highlands—lush hills or mountains whose peaks rose toward the warming rays of the sun. In summer they found cool relief in shady stands of cottonwood trees, whose roots drew nourishment from the creeks that snaked through this mostly barren area. The Apache were also careful to build sites that could easily be defended against attackers.

The dry climate of the Southwest dictated the clothing worn by the Apache. Women wore skirts; men wore breechcloths. Both items have been described by Ralph Ogle in *Federal Control of the Western Apache*: "The breechcloth was about two yards long. It passed between the legs and hung over the belt in front and behind, the rear part almost

Apache women liked layered necklaces and beaded hairpieces, such as those worn by this resident of the San Carlos Reservation. In summer, Apache men often went bare chested.

reaching the ground. A common buckskin skirt was composed of two buckskins hung over a belt, one in front and the other behind in the form of a kilt. The edges of the skirt were cut in deep fringe." Men and women alike wore knee-high moccasins whose folds served as pockets. The soles, which had to be durable, were made from undressed hides, and the toes were upturned. These unique shoes caused another Indian people, the Comanche, to refer to the Apache as *Tá-ashi*, or "Turned-up."

The climate also influenced the Apache diet. Precipitation was scant in this region. A year's rainfall seldom surpassed 20 inches and often did not reach 10. Consequently, little vegetation grew in the plains. Some grasses thrived, but only because they were hardy enough to withstand the climatic extremes of the sudden storms, long droughts, and the fires that sometimes seared the land.

The Apache seldom farmed, not only because the climate discouraged it but also because they were frequently on the move and unlikely to linger long enough in one place to nurture their crops. Some Apache did cultivate the land, however. The Western Apache grew maize (corn), beans, and squash and even remained near their crops for part of the year. Still, the harvest provided only 20 percent of their diet.

The Apache fared better as hunters. Game was plentiful in the Southwest, and most bands included meat in their diet. They savored the meat of ante-lope, deer, hare, and even rodents, which they hunted skillfully with bows and arrows. The Kiowa, Lipan, and Chiricahua bands all hunted buffalo and prepared its meat in many ways— boiled, baked, roasted, even raw. They set aside some of the flesh to be dried on racks, then eaten as jerky. Buffalo blood thickened stews, soups, and puddings. The Apache used more than just the flesh of the animals they killed. Buffalo hide could be sewn into sturdy bags, moccasins, robes, and more. Women made blankets and scarves from buffalo hide, and warriors made shields, lariats, and cords.

Women contributed to the food supply by gathering fruits, vegetables,

An Apache woman stretches a hide on the ground, after first stripping away the remaining flesh and fur—a process that took several days.

roots, and nuts that grew wild, including strawberries, grapes, and mulberries; onions, potatoes, and mesquite beans; piñon nuts and walnuts; and sunflower seeds and acorns. These foodstuffs constituted a major portion of the diet: 40 percent among the Western Apache, the most agricultural of the bands.

One method of obtaining food was raiding, which the Apache viewed as a life-sustaining enterprise, like hunting and food gathering. They raided primarily to steal food, preferably livestock, but they also made off with weapons, supplies, and children, whom they accepted into the band and raised as their own. Before the Spaniards introduced horses to the Apache in the 16th century, raiding warriors traveled by foot. Their depredations were the major cause of discord between Apache bands and other Indians and would later cause friction with non-Indian settlers.

The Apache developed a distinct social organization. Its fundamental unit was the family. Unlike contemporary American households, which usually consist only of parents and children,

After the Spaniards introduced horses to the Southwest, the Apache used them as pack animals, loading them with their belongings when they changed campsites.

Apache home life was centered on the extended family. Its members included the various blood relations of the parents and their offspring—grandparents and grandchildren, cousins, aunts and uncles, nephews and nieces.

In Apache culture these persons constituted a kind of miniature society that lived in adjacent wickiups, shared tasks such as hunting and gathering, and assisted each other in times of stress. An important figure was the mother-in-law, who supervised much social activity. Sons-in-law, for instance, brought her game they had killed. She cooked and apportioned it to others in the group.

Marriage was a crucial event because it redistributed males among different families. In the Jicarilla culture, when a couple decided to marry, the suitor's relatives bestowed gifts upon the relatives of his intended bride. And in all the bands, the relatives had to agree to any marriage. Once the match was approved, the wedding took place. It involved little ceremony. A large basin made of buffalo hide was carried to a secluded place and filled with fresh water. The bride and groom stepped into it, held hands, and awaited the appearance of both sets of parents, who had to acknowledge the matrimony. Afterward the party walked together to the bride's camp and joined a public dance.

The wedded couple took up residence near the wife's relatives, and the husband provided for them and fulfilled their wishes. This relationship

Apache infants spent most of their first six months in a cradleboard, such as this one. Buckskin covers its frame and hood.

continued even if the wife died. On such an occasion, the widower mourned for a year, then married one of his wife's sisters or cousins. If the husband died first, his widow was expected to marry one of his brothers or cousins.

Despite the close bonds formed between spouses and their in-laws, the Apache allowed for divorce. Incompatibility and infidelity could end a marriage, as could laziness, bickering, and jealousy. If a married woman misbe-

Apache women wove splendid baskets out of the differently colored leaves of the yucca plant.

named for some natural feature of the landscape they inhabited. Clan names included Water at the Foot of Hill People, Between Two Hills People, White Water People, and In the Rocks People. Members of the same clan could not marry each other.

Within the family, tasks were generally divided along gender lines, with some crossing over. Hunting, for example, was a male activity, but Lipan women helped track down rabbits and antelope, and men in the various tribes sometimes helped pick berries and other fruits. Similarly, women tanned hides, but men assisted with large or heavy skins, such as those removed from the carcasses of slain buffalo and antelope. Women raised children, but fathers and male relatives often pitched in. Sewing, however, was strictly women's work, as was gathering brush for fires and cooking. Men repaired their own hunting weapons adeptly, and Apache warriors were known for fashioning some of the finest arrows, arrowheads, and lances ever produced by American Indians.

When several extended families merged, they formed a local group. Day to day, the group unit functioned like the extended families and was led by the male heads of each. When a serious issue—such as dwindling resources or enemy threats—faced the group, the family heads convened in a council that discussed the problem and planned a strategy. The council itself was led by an inner circle composed not only of family heads but also of other men

haved, her husband left the camp. In the event her family recognized him as a good provider, they would make an effort to keep him happy by straightening out his wife. If her family had no use for him, they drove him away.

As we might expect from a group that so highly valued the wife's family, the Apache were matrilineal—that is, they traced their descent through their mother. In some groups, families connected by common ancestors constituted a clan. The Western Apache, for example, comprised 60 clans, most

Local leader Antonio Maria and his wife both wear European-style shirts in this photo—probably from the late 19th century. Even after the Apache were introduced to cloth, they seldom wove it themselves, preferring to trade for it.

noted for bravery, wealth, or wisdom. The most dominant man among those in the inner circle served as the group's top leader.

Local groups were not always large enough or strong enough to solve all the problems that faced them. Thus, they merged to form yet a larger union, the band, which usually contained between 200 to 300 people. It too had an inner council, and its members were the main leaders of the individual groups. The most respected of these leaders dominated the band, just as the local leaders dominated the groups and the family head dominated the extended family.

The band council probably functioned differently from the group council. It seems that the local-group council focused on such everyday matters as locating ideal places to hunt, whereas the band council was more concerned with organizing raiding parties and planning for war. Both councils, however, worked democratically. All members expressed opinions and tried to achieve a consensus, so that everyone shared in the final decision and helped carry it out. Even a towering figure such as Cochise, the 19th-century Chiricahua chief, consulted with his council before guiding his band into action.

Leaders had many responsibilities. They settled disputes between competing families and persons and made sure that the band or group worked harmoniously to hunt and gather food. Their most important task was giving advice. Indeed the Chiricahua word for leader, *nantà*, translates as "he who talks or advises." One 20th-century Apache, quoted in Morris Opler's *An Apache Life-way*, enumerated the qualities of the ideal leader:

> The leader is supposed to talk to his people. He is supposed to be sympathetic and tell them how to live, sympathetic in the sense of giving out horses and valuables to those who need them. The leader is supposed to give something to eat to everyone who comes around [in need]. He has control in time of war. You can't disobey him. The leader advises people to help the unfortunate, to give to those whose luck is bad. He advises against fights in the camps; he doesn't want any quarrels within the group. He advises the people to be on the lookout all the time. He may request that a ceremony be performed by a shaman [a healer] for the benefit of the men during a raid. If the leader is advised by the shaman as a result of such a ceremony to do this or that, he carries out what the power tells him to do. A man must be wealthy and have a big following to be a chief.

An Apache leader, then, had to possess many qualities—wealth, wisdom, sympathy, and strength. He had to speak well but also be willing to listen. He had to reach the right decision and command enough loyalty to enforce it. Often chiefs acquired leadership through family connections. The brothers or sons of a leader had an inside track on acquiring the mantle themselves. Yet—as in other societies—being born into the right family was never enough. Ultimately, leaders rose to eminence by acclaim.

At least several times a week, the leader assembled his group and ad-dressed it from a prominent place—atop a rock or hill. Even when there was little news to report, the leader kept in touch with his people and offered advice meant to improve their lives. In *The Social Organization of the Western Apache*, anthropologist Grenville Goodwin provides an example of a typical speech:

A Tonto couple—of the Western Apache—poses with their two infants. Family tasks were generally divided along gender lines. Women raised the children, for example, but fathers often pitched in.

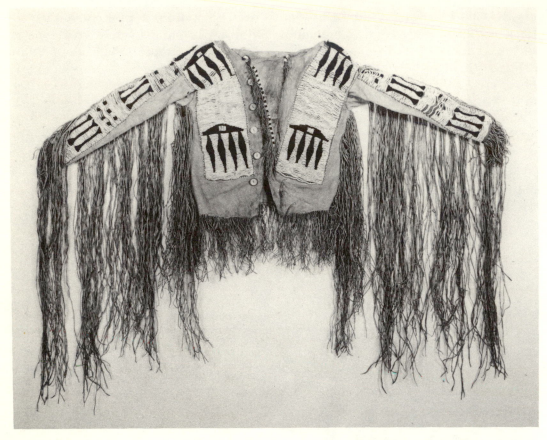

Fine beadwork covers this buckskin shirt. Fringes were usually sewn into the sleeves with deer sinew.

Do not be lazy. Even if there is a deep canyon or a steep place to climb, you must go up it. Thus, it will be easy for you to [track down and kill] deer. If any of you go out hunting this morning . . . , look after yourselves [when] you are alone. When you trail deer you may step on a rock. If the rock slips from under you, you may fall and get hurt. If there is a thick growth of trees ahead of you, don't go in it. There might be a lion in a tree ready to attack you.

In addition to advising the men on hunting methods, leaders took charge of the riskier business of raiding. Raids were staged by warriors who volunteered for the assignment, which was considered a privilege. If the attack was successful—that is, if the men made off with plunder (livestock and weapons) and no Apache lives were lost—the warriors usually held a feast and distributed some of the booty among the rest of the group.

An even more dangerous enterprise was warfare, which for centuries remained a crucial part of Apache existence. Most battles were undertaken to avenge the death of group members, who usually were killed during raids. The slain warrior's family led the way during battle. Costumed dancers called on other warriors, outside the family, to join the expedition. The head of the aggrieved family acted as leader, though he consulted with other men and might even submit to the authority of another, more respected leader. Before men departed to engage in battle, the community summoned the assistance of divine spirits by performing a dance in which the men took the part of Child of the Water and the women took the part of White-painted Woman, two mythological figures said to have founded the Apache nation. Anyone whom they opposed was considered a monster and the enemy of all human life. The dance reminded warriors that they sallied forth to engage no mere opponents but the would-be destroyers of their entire blessed race.

During peacetime, the Apache lived a regulated existence. They had no laws, judges, police, or jails, but they obeyed a code of honor passed on from one generation to the next. As a 20th-century Apache explained to researcher Morris Opler:

> Good conduct is the result of obeying the customs, and it is up to the person. . . . A man would come to a bad end in the old days [if] he violated the customs. . . . If you obey all the rules, you get along all right. . . . But if a person doesn't take hold of the customs, if he cuts loose, if he doesn't treat other people right, he has no chance. Then the others do not help him. He is alone. He is bound to come to a bad end and perhaps be killed. A person just has to observe certain things. They aren't laws—they are so strong we don't need laws. ▲

The Chiricahua warrior Geronimo was also a shaman, or healer.
Here he wears a ceremonial headdress and a European-style shirt.

POWER
AND
PORTENT

Rules of conduct invariably rest on a deep foundation of spiritual belief. Such was the case with the Apache. Edward Curtis states in *The North American Indian*, a multivolume work published in 1930, that "the Apache is inherently devoutly religious; his life is completely molded by his religious beliefs. From his morning prayers to the rising sun, through the hours, the days and the months—throughout life itself—every act has some religious significance."

The Apache did not build religious institutions, but they incorporated spirituality into their everyday life. The 19th-century Chiricahua leader Geronimo, who also served the role of healer, explained his band's religious attitude in *Geronimo's Story of His Life*:

> We had no churches, no religious organizations, no sabbath day, no holidays, and yet we worshipped. Sometimes the whole tribe would assemble to sing and pray; sometimes in a smaller number, perhaps only two or three. . . . Sometimes we prayed in silence; sometimes each one prayed aloud; sometimes an aged person prayed for all of us.

According to the Apache, the universe was imbued with power, which they regarded as a spiritual substance or cosmic force. Every object, idea, and person contained elements of power; it was present everywhere, like air. Sometimes power served good purposes, breathing vitality into living things. But power was equally responsible for disease and death, and good power could degenerate into bad. Though invisible, power could be discerned easily and in a variety of ways. Someone who experienced muscle tremors, for instance, took them as physical evidence of power. Dreams also conveyed power. And power could be obtained more directly on occasions in which it sought out human contacts, who became the vehicle of its wishes.

These encounters between a person and power could be dangerous and often put the person to a test. An Apache quoted by Morris Opler described possible reactions to such a meeting:

> I might reply to the power when it comes, "I'm a poor fellow, and there are many other people here good enough for that, let me alone. I don't want your ceremony!". . . It is said that some fellows have done that. They claim it is more dangerous to take it than to refuse it sometimes. They say some power might help you nicely for several years and then begin a lot of trouble. You might have to sacrifice your friends. Then if you refuse you might get killed yourself. But, if I am not afraid and am interested in this power and this ceremony, I will go up [the mountain] the next morning. Then it will appear in the form of a person or as a spirit. "Well," it will say, "you will be a shaman and have power from the sun."

After making its presence known by speech, power later appeared in human form and spoke to the recipient. If he or she agreed to accept the offered power, then it revealed the details of a ceremony that only it could authorize.

The goodwill of power was cultivated in ceremonies supervised by religious figures—shamans and priests. Shamans, older men and sometimes women, rose to eminence by displaying unique spiritual gifts, especially the ability to communicate with supernatural beings. Hence, they served as mediums, conveying the hidden wishes of the sacred forces. Priests arrived at their post more formally, through inheritance and the diligent study of standard ritual knowledge taught by their elders. Instead of giving voice to the desires of the gods, these religious men functioned as intermediaries between the divine will and the mortal population.

Power, an elusive substance, freely defied mortal attempts to harness it, especially if a shaman ran afoul of it. As one Apache has put it: "The old people say that a shaman often falls out with his own power. Many stories have been told about that, all of them true. After many years, the power will ask some shamans to sacrifice some of their best friends or the very ones they love best in the family."

Power could also render useful services. It could weaken enemies, protect groups from attack, even ward off arrows and bullets. Power was said to enable shamans to locate missing objects, root out hidden adversaries, and control the water supply and other natural phenomena. Its most beneficial service was allowing shamans to diagnose and cure illness.

This was done in ceremonies that, like other Apache activities, acknowledged their closeness to nature. Many Apache rituals, for example, involved pollen. Pollen represented the life-force, fertility, and beauty. In the healing ceremony, it represented health, the condition that the patient sought to recapture.

Patients usually visited the shaman at his home and offered him a gift, sometimes a single cigarette, as payment for his services. This photo shows a shaman relaxing with his family.

The healing ceremony began with an event attended by the patient, his or her relatives, and other members of the local group. The sufferer initiated the proceedings by formally approaching the healer with a request for aid. He then spoke the name of the shaman and his family and demonstrated his respect and faith by marking the healer with pollen. Next he traced a cross on the shaman's right foot, sprinkled other parts of his body with pollen, and drew a second cross, this time on the left foot. Sometimes, the suppliant also gave the healer gifts, even a single cigarette. By accepting the present, or smoking the cigarette, the shaman indicated his willingness to take the case.

The shaman then took over. An Apache explained to Morris Opler what one such healer did. First he rolled a cigarette, blew smoke in the four cardinal directions—which were considered sacred—and said, "May it be well." Then he called upon his power. "This woman is in poor health. I want her to live. She has been searching for something good. This evening I hope that what is wrong with her will disappear and that she will have a good life. . . . You must do right now what you promised me to do. Your power must go into the life of this poor woman.''

Next, the shaman explained the origin and meaning of this particular ceremony, and he and the sick person marked one another with pollen. The healer then sang and prayed to his power, who might inform him that he had correctly diagnosed the illness and should proceed with his cure.

The ceremony was repeated on four consecutive nights. It began at dark and

In this photo, taken in 1946, a masked dancer pays tribute to Apache warriors who served in World War II.

continued until midnight, when everyone dined on food provided by the patient's relatives. At the conclusion of the fourth night, the healer sucked out poison supposedly planted in the patient by an evil shaman or witch and spat it into a fire. He then would impose restrictions on the patient, often dietary, such as a prohibition against eating liver. The healer might also give a protective charm to the suppliant.

Every Apache band but the Kiowa celebrated the Mountain Spirits, originally part of the religion practiced by the Pueblo, another southwestern people. The Mountain Spirits generally represented good power and could protect people from illness. They were invoked in a healing ceremony similar to the one described above, except that it used masked dancers.

As with the ceremony already described, the patient approached the shaman and formally presented his case. He also lavished gifts on the healer and marked him with pollen. By throwing himself on the mercy of the shaman, the patient sought his pity, the emotion that led the healer to salve the wound. If the shaman accepted the case, he selected four men to act as masked dancers and then painted them in an elaborate style. Meanwhile, the patient's relatives built a corral with a fire burning in the center and openings in the structure facing in each direction. The patient was then placed in the corral to await the dancers.

Healers donned special clothing to perform their services. Shown here are items worn by Chiricahua shamans: a necklace with a wooden "medicine" cross (left) and a painted buckskin whose many crosses may symbolize the four cardinal directions.

Drums sounded as the dancers approached from the east, trailing the shaman, who sang and danced as the troupe entered. He stepped toward the flame, circled it clockwise, then retraced his steps toward the east. The four dancers circled the fire four times, assumed positions of worship, and followed the shaman to the ailing supplicant, who daubed them with paint. Next the shaman approached the patient, asked where he hurt, and then directed the dancers to execute a series of steps four times. After the last series, the lead dancer ceremonially exhaled in every direction in order to blow the illness away. The other dancers did likewise, then left the corral.

This ceremony was repeated, with slight variations, for three more nights. On the second or third night, the healer might check the patient's progress. He pressed abalone—a mollusk with a spiral shell—against the patient's forehead. If the abalone stuck, his chances of recovery were good. If not, he faced prolonged illness. In either case, the ceremony continued for the full four nights. After a favorable prognosis, the shaman prescribed remedies. He might instruct the patient to avoid certain foods. He also warned the patient that if he violated these restrictions, disease would recur. If the outlook seemed bad, the shaman prayed for the afflicted person until he recovered. Sometimes this ceremony was performed on a larger scale to benefit the whole community.

Just as the Apache believed in the life-force, so they believed that death held mysterious powers. When someone died, his or her relatives began a period of mourning. They wailed, cut their hair, and donned old clothing. Older relatives then prepared the corpse for burial. Some Apache were afraid to touch dead bodies and enlisted strangers or captives to lay them to rest. Others enacted a burial ritual that could have originated no earlier than the mid-16th century, when the Spaniards introduced the Apache to horses. In this ritual, horses served as hearses. Relatives of the dead person loaded up a horse with the body of the dead person, along with his personal possessions, and led it away from the camp. They hid the dead person among crevices in the rocks, then destroyed most of the belongings, entombing the remainder much as the ancient Egyptians buried the dead along with their cherished goods. The burial party slew the horse and returned to camp, where they cleansed themselves and burned their ritual clothing.

According to Apache mythology, when someone died, his or her body released a spirit that was guided into the underworld by the ghosts of dead relatives. The Lipan, Jicarilla, and Western Apache all believed the underworld consisted of two sections. One was a pleasant green place inhabited by the ghosts of virtuous people. The other was a barren place inhabited by the ghosts of witches.

To hasten the ghost's departure, living relatives conducted a formal funeral service. It had to be observed to the letter. Otherwise the ghost might decide to remain among the living and cause them harm. Even a ghost properly banished to the underworld might return to wreak sickness and death on the living. Thus, every effort was made to hold the dead at bay—even thinking about the dead, it was believed, encouraged ghosts to return. The relatives of the deceased isolated themselves for a while from the rest of the band and avoided social functions. An entire group might move camp because ghosts were thought to favor familiar places.

But nothing guaranteed that ghosts would remain in the underworld. Ghosts grew lonely there and longed for human company. They returned to find companions whom they could transport back with them. Thus, the Apache believed that seeing a ghost doomed one to death. The ghosts of witches who had been exposed and burned alive were the most frightening of all. The Lipan, Jicarilla, and Chirica-

THE SLAYING OF THE MONSTERS

Apache mythology describes the adventures of ancient gods, humans, and animals in order to explain the creation of the world and how it operates. Although each Apache tribe has its own unique stories, three culture heroes are common to all Apache mythology: White-painted Woman, Killer of Enemies, and Child of the Water.

One myth explains how, long ago, Child of the Water made the earth safe by killing four monsters who preyed on human beings. In the beginning, White-painted Woman and Killer of Enemies, who was either her brother or son, lived together on the earth. They were tormented by monsters, especially Owl-man Giant, who stole the deer meat shot with bow and arrow by Killer of Enemies. One day when White-painted Woman was praying for the monsters to leave them alone, the spirit known as Life Giver came to her in the form of rain and lightning and told her she would have a baby who would be called Child of the Water. The spirit warned White-painted Woman that she must protect the baby from Owl-man Giant. Through her cunning, White-painted Woman kept the child safe.

One day, while he was still a boy, Child of the Water told his mother that he was ready to leave her to kill the monsters. White-painted Woman fashioned him a wooden bow and grama-grass arrows and let him venture out to hunt deer with Killer of Enemies. After they had killed their first deer, Owl-man Giant came to take the meat away. But Child of the Water refused to give it up. The opponents agreed to a contest. Each would be allowed to shoot four arrows. Owl-man Giant was to shoot first. But before he began, lightning flashed all around and a blue rock appeared at the feet of Child of the Water. The rock spoke, saying that Child of the Water should pick it up and use it as a charm. The boy did and waited for Owl-man Giant to shoot his arrows. They were made of sharp, large-pointed logs. The first arrow flew over Child of the Water's head. The second landed at his feet. The third and fourth missed him on either side.

Then it was Child of the Water's turn. Owl-man Giant wore four coats of flint to protect his chest and picked up a rock to try to deflect the arrows, as Child of the Water had done. But the first three arrows that Child of the Water shot knocked off a coat of flint, and the fourth pierced Owl-man Giant's heart.

Killer of Enemies and Child of the Water returned to White-painted Woman, who danced and sang with happiness. Child of the Water then went out again on further hunts. He killed the Buffalo Monster, then the Eagle Monster, and finally the Antelope Monster. The earth was now safe, and the human population began to grow. Thus, the Apache regard Child of the Water as their divine ancestor.

hua also feared the ghosts of enemies. Ghosts chose nighttime to make their appearance. Sometimes they emerged from dreams or took the shape of owls or coyotes. Even steely Apache warriors quaked at the hooting of owls.

Not all rituals involved death and disease. Others, equally important, saluted life and health. One acknowledged the passage of young girls into puberty—the time when they were physically mature enough to bear children. This ceremony bespoke the Apache belief that the desire for fertility and beauty required a struggle with the earth, which yielded fruit only grudgingly, a desert world covered with the spiny skeletons of cacti and century plants—which flower only once, then die.

Two members of the band played important roles in this ceremony. There was an attendant, an older woman, often with shamanistic gifts, who stayed with the initiate throughout the rite. A second functionary was the singer, usually an old man. Preparations for the girl's initiation began before the onset of menstruation. The girl's female relatives sewed and decorated an elaborate costume meant to duplicate the garb worn by White-painted Woman, the mythological figure said to have created the ceremony ushering girls into womanhood during her mortal time on earth.

The girl took on the role of White-painted Woman because the Apache associated the fertility of a budding woman with the fruitfulness of the

Apache lore holds that ghosts choose to appear at night and often take the shape of nocturnal creatures, such as coyotes or owls.

earth. Thus, the initiate gained godlike power and blessed the Apache people by giving birth to new members and by linking the existing members with the procreative process. Before sunrise on the first day of the ceremony, an attendant dressed the young girl—referred to during the proceedings as White-painted Woman—in her finery and gave her precise instructions. Another attendant then initiated preparations for the construction of a tipi that duplicated the dwelling of White-painted Woman. This shelter was built at sunrise while songs were sung. When the singer named divine figures, the attendant cried out, simulating the cries emitted by White-painted Woman when Child of the Water returned victorious from his battle with Giant and other monsters.

As the first day ended, the attendant and the young girl entered the shelter and were marked with pollen. The attendant supervised a complex ritual. She placed an animal skin on the ground near the southeast corner of the tipi, where the girl knelt facing a basket filled with pollen and other objects. Next the attendant offered the pollen to the four directions, painted the girl, and was painted by her in return. She then positioned her on the skin, face down, with her head pointing east, toward sunrise, and massaged her, praying the girl would be virtuous and mannerly. The girl rose, and the attendant painted four footprints of pollen on the animal skin. The girl then trod in these steps, again toward the east, which promised good health and luck.

This solemn ritual gave way to more public activities in the afternoon. There was dancing, and some people ap-

Many Apache still practice the ancestral puberty rite, which ushers girls into womanhood. Here an attendant sprinkles the initiate with pollen, a symbol of procreation.

An initiate appears before the singer, who blesses her and also blesses ceremonial food held by an onlooker. A feast concludes the ceremony; the girl is then eligible to marry.

proached the girl to request that she help the ill because her emergent womanhood instilled her with healing powers. At night masked dancers appeared. They worshiped a campfire and sometimes circled and blessed the ceremonial tipi. They danced to drive away sickness, then to amuse and entertain the people gathered for the occasion. Inside the tipi, the singer performed songs meant to guide the young initiate into a long, successful life.

These proceedings continued for four days and nights. On the last night, the activities within the tipi lasted till dawn. When the sun rose, the singer sang four songs, faced east, and painted his own face and head. He then painted the girl. He sang once again and drew a sun symbol on his left palm, then pointed his palm toward the rising sun. As its first rays struck the girl, the singer rubbed his painted hand on her head, then gripped a brush made of an eagle feather and grama grass and painted her head with white clay. He marked the onlookers with pollen, and also marked ceremonial food brought before him. Everyone ate and the singer and girl left the tipi. She followed a path that was marked with pollen on an animal skin, then returned for the last time to the tipi, which was knocked down by others in the group. The assembly tossed presents in the air and children scrambled for them. The initiate and her female attendant retired from the group for four days of recovery. The girl returned to her parents' dwelling eligible for marriage.

An equivalent ritual celebrated the arrival of boys at the threshold of manhood, when they became warriors and were permitted to marry. Preparations began in boyhood with rigorous physical training supervised at first by the boy's father and male relatives, who ordered him to practice running and also to perform feats that tested his strength and endurance—all for the purpose of honing his battle skills. Before they became warriors, youngsters accompanied their elders on raids. This exposed them to the dangers of the life that awaited them.

Daily life included instruction from older men in the ways of war. As one Apache remembered, "They told me to sleep in a place from which I could get to cover quickly. And they told me 'even if it is a hot day, don't go to the deep shade. Go under a little bush in the open or under grass. The first place a Mexican or another Indian or a wild animal looks when it comes along is the shade, and there you are. If you are in the tall grass and hear something, just pick some grass up, hold it before you, and look through it. Then it will be hard to see you, especially from a distance. If you are out where the brush is heavy and you want to conceal yourself without moving, just take a branch which is to the right or left and pull it in front of you.' " When a young man reached puberty, he was ready for his formal initiation. First he had to study a special sacred language composed of about 80 phrases. For example, the word for *heart* translated as "that by means of which I live," and the word for *pollen* meant "becoming life."

The Apache carried out these and all such rituals as meticulously as possible, although they knew full well that there was no sure way of staving off ill fortune. When it arose, they usually placed the blame on witchcraft practiced by evil shamans. As one Apache explained to Morris Opler:

There are lots of ways to [distinguish] a witch from a shaman, though most people who have much power will have both kinds [good and evil]. The truth is [that] a person is a shaman if he uses his power for good, and a witch if he uses it for evil. You have to guess [which he is] by what happens; you have to use your own judgment. Therefore, there are a good many people who look at the same person differently.

The ambiguity, then, originated in the unpredictable nature of power itself, which could suddenly veer from good to evil, benefiting the group one day, plaguing it the next. Witchcraft was hard to detect because no one owned up to it. By definition, it unfolded secretly, and the community could only guess when it had been practiced. An Apache described some telltale signs to Morris Opler:

Sometimes witching is done with hair or with a rib and hair done up in buckskin. This is their arrow. . . . They shoot these objects into the body of the one they are making sick. . . . Few shamans try to take objects out of a sick person's body which have been placed there through evil influence. It is dangerous and most shamans are afraid. Sometimes the glance, the thought, or the speech of a witch will cause evil influence. And a witch can often work through [obtaining] some part of the man whom it wants to harm, such as hair or nail parings.

White Americans often had a lurid view of Indian rites. This 19th-century illustration by Frederic Remington shows two men cowering as a shaman contacts the spirits of their ancestors.

The ability of witches to accomplish their evil purposes by a glance, speech, or even a thought, the Apache believed, enabled them to defy detection and added to their power. Hence, Apache remained on the alert for subtle clues to witchcraft. Strange behavior, for instance, was thought to identify a witch. If a shaman spoke or dressed oddly or employed unusual healing charms he might arouse suspicion.

Whenever the Apache suspected a witch was among them, they turned to powerful shamans, for it was believed only they could neutralize or defeat witchcraft. During the healing ceremony, for instance, when shamans discerned the cause of illness, they lured the witch into a contest of good and evil. Once a witch came under suspicion the Apache acted quickly, as one man explained to Opler:

They string the witch up by the wrists so his feet are off the ground. The witch has to tell whom he witched. The confession is good evidence. . . . They never let [him] go if they prove [he is wicked]. Then a fire is built under the witch, and he is burned. Burning destroys a witch's power for future harm, but what he has already accomplished is not undone. Witches do not [die] quickly; they keep on living a long time.

If these harsh methods sound familiar, it is because they resemble those employed by Christians in Europe and in the American colonies. In the 15th century the Spanish Inquisition—the result of an effort to convert an entire nation to the Roman Catholic faith—resulted in mass burnings of alleged witches. Sometimes a hundred might be set ablaze in a one-day ceremony called *auto-da-fe*. And just as the Apache singled out people who used unusual charms—those who devised unique ways of healing—so some Christians pounced on people who dared to engage in scientific experiments that clashed with the teachings of the Roman Catholic church. Protestants, too, executed witches. In 1692, 20 were hanged by Puritans in the colonial town of Salem, Massachusetts.

Europeans would have been appalled by the comparison of their own "civilized" culture to that of a "barbaric" Indian tribe. They might have bridled no less at the suggestion that they held beliefs as mysterious as the Apache belief in shamans and pollen. Yet their very different forms of faith would meet—and clash—in a dramatic episode that helped shape American history. ▲

In 1541, Francisco Vásquez de Coronado (holding sword) became the first white man to reach the Missouri River.

THE
FIRST
STRANGERS

In 1526, some three decades after Christopher Columbus and his crew first stumbled onto the North American continent, Charles V, the king of Spain, granted a charter to explorer Pánfilo de Narvaez authorizing him to conquer and colonize a vast area of the New World. Narvaez left the port of Sanlucar in June 1527 with 5 ships and a crew of 600. The voyage across the Atlantic Ocean lasted almost a year, as storms blew the ships off course. Many men had deserted by the spring of 1528, when the expedition sailed up the Gulf of Mexico and anchored in Tampa Bay, near present-day St. Petersburg, Florida.

Narvaez ordered the ships to press on up the gulf, toward Mexico. He then disembarked with 300 men, who traveled inland by foot in search of gold, which they believed existed abundantly in this unknown land. Instead they found Apalachee Indians, whose resentment of the intruders forced Narvaez to retreat. Decimated by mal-

nutrition and disease, his forces struggled back to the coast, but when they arrived no ships lay at anchor. In panic, the Spaniards hastily chopped down trees and fashioned the trunks into planks, riveting them together with spurs they plucked off their boots. For sails and rigging they used horse hides. In short order they had five rough-hewn boats. They set sail on a westward voyage along the Gulf Coast toward Mexico, but as they drew near the coast of what is now Galveston, Texas, a gale destroyed craft and crew.

Only four men survived: Álvar Núñez Cabeza de Vaca, Alonso del Castillo Maldonado, Andrés Dorantes de Carranco, and his black slave, Estevanico. They clambered ashore, where they were captured by Indians and held for six years. At last they escaped and struggled across the parched landscape of Texas, toward colonies in Mexico established by the Spanish some years earlier. Their trek took more than a year. On the way they encountered buf-

Cabeza de Vaca survived a shipwreck off the Texas coast, was imprisoned for six years by Indians, and then trekked across the desert. Here a friendly Indian guides him toward Mexico.

falo—the first Europeans to do so—and friendlier Indians (including Apache). These peoples hailed the four foreigners as healers and traders, treated them like kings, and escorted them to their destination, Mexico City, in March 1536. The Spaniards had recently established a colony there after destroying the native Aztec culture.

Welcomed into this Spanish colony near the southern end of Mexico, Cabeza de Vaca and his companions regaled their countrymen with tales of their wanderings. They described the turquoise, buffalo-hide robes, and cotton blankets they had seen in the possession of Indians who had gotten them by trading with great cities to the north. The weary travelers described the gold and other precious metals they had seen. Finally, they told of seven rich cities whose walls glittered with emeralds. Cabeza de Vaca and the others had not actually seen these cities, but they had heard of them from the Indians they had met on their journey.

The account of the seven cities gripped the imagination of Mendoza, the viceroy, or top official, in Mexico, who fancifully connected it with a time-worn Spanish legend. The tale originated in the 8th century, when the Moors, a people from northern Africa, invaded the Iberian Peninsula and

(continued on page 57)

PRACTICAL ARTISTRY

The Apache valued craftwork that joined beauty with utility. Women wove eye-catching baskets and clothing, and men spent many hours fashioning superb weapons, such as bows and arrows.

Arrows were usually made of cane or reed, cut to a length of about 30 inches and straightened between the teeth of the warrior. Bows took longer to make. First the warrior found a hardwood branch—often mulberry or oak—carefully bent it, placed it in hot ashes, and then cured it for about 10 days. A top-notch bow could send an arrow 150 yards and was ideal for hunting large, swift game such as antelope, elk, and deer.

The choicest game was deer, which provided tasty meat as well as hides that women turned into buckskin, using a difficult process. The first step was for the woman to scrape the hide of remaining flesh with a stone or sharpened bone. She then mixed steamed deer fat and brains into a tanning paste, which she kneaded into the hide until it softened. She hung it to dry overnight, and the next morning she awoke early to pull and stretch the tough hide. By noon she had buckskin that could be tailored into shirts, leggings, dresses, moccasins, headdresses, and accessories—all painted with hues extracted from boiled roots (yellows), mahogany bark (reds), and walnut juice (browns).

White Mountain Apache made the attached quiver and bow case shown here. The practice of joining the two items originated with the Chiricahua.

49

Crosses often symbolized
the four prime directions.
The mask at top left has a
decorative cross-shaped
attachment made of
deerskin. On the mask at
left, crosses are inscribed
within circles.

Some Apache warriors attached antelope horns to their headdresses.

Eagle feathers top this warrior's headdress, which was held in place by a beaded chin strap.

The hide garment at left shows mirror images of masked figures and serpents. The skin at center depicts masked dancers circling a fire before three rings of observers.

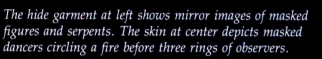

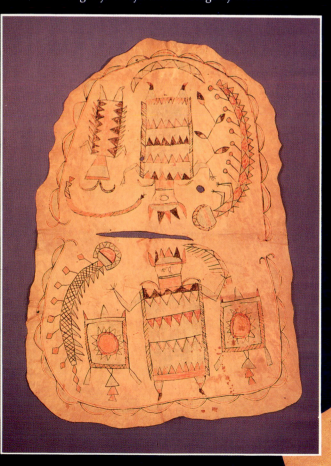

Whites introduced playing cards to the Apache, who developed a rawhide deck faced with stick figures instead of numbers. The exact meaning of these pictographs is unknown.

Scenes of daily life adorn the skin at lower right.

53

A Mescalero woman sewed this fringed and beaded dress.

This painted bag with shoulder strap was made by a Chiricahua.

Even in cold weather, Apache men needed freedom of movement and thus wore round-necked, fringed tunics.

Shields made of cowhide were wetted and molded into shape, and then hardened over coals. A century plant adorns this painted shield.

(continued from page 48)

overran Spain and Portugal. The Moors, who practiced Islam, persecuted Spain's population of Roman Catholics. Led by seven bishops, some of the Catholics fled in boats that sailed westward into the uncharted and mysterious Ocean Sea (the Atlantic). Legend had it that these bishops discovered a lush island stocked with food and studded with jewels and gold. The bishops named this paradise Antilla, and each of the seven built his own city there.

In later centuries, Spanish adventurers set out for Antilla, but none found it, and its fabled cities remained shrouded in mystery. But Cabeza de Vaca's account meshed with the legend of the cities—even if he had traveled through a place no 8th-century Spaniards could ever have visited—and the viceroy of Mexico wanted to send an expedition north to find them. Mendoza tried to entice Cabeza de Vaca and the other survivors to head the expedition, but they all spurned the offer. The viceroy located another candidate, Friar Marcos de Niza, a well-traveled missionary. He had just arrived in the colony after seven years of traveling in Santo Domingo (today the Dominican Republic), Guatemala, and other distant places in the Southern Hemisphere. Friar Marcos, according to John Terrell's *Apache Chronicle*, "display[ed] a craving for adventure and sightseeing which challenged his love for his work as a missionary." He jumped at Mendoza's offer to set off in search of the seven lost cities. The viceroy sent a letter to the king of Spain requesting permission to employ Friar Marcos in this manner.

In September 1538, Mendoza received royal approval, and he instructed Marcos and his guide, the slave Estevanico, to proceed to the west coast of Mexico in the company of Don Francisco Vásquez de Coronado, who was headed there to assume his duties as governor of Nueva Galicia. The trio reached that province's capital, Compostela, in December. Friar Marcos and Estevanico then waited for the warmth of spring before resuming their journey.

March came and the travelers set off, heading north. Three weeks later, the pair reached the village of Vacapan, where the friar remained to celebrate Easter. He told Estevanico, who was not a Christian, to continue the journey and gave him precise instructions. Estevanico should proceed no farther than 50 or 60 leagues (about 150 miles). If he discovered something of importance, he was to send back a cross the length of his palm. If he found out something of great importance, the cross should be two palms long. If he stumbled on something truly extraordinary, he should send back a large cross.

Just before Easter, Estevanico and several Indian guides departed Vacapan. For nearly a week, Friar Marcos heard nothing. Then some of the advance party returned to the village bearing a mammoth cross and a message from Estevanico urging Friar Marcos to

Diego Hurtado de Mendoza, the viceroy of Mexico, confused Cabeza de Vaca's account of Indian pueblos with an 8th-century Spanish legend about seven fabulous cities.

rendezvous with him. Before the friar left, another cross arrived. Marcos set off with a party of his own, but when he arrived at the appointed village, Estevanico was not there.

The slave had pressed ahead on his own. He had passed through numerous Apache camps, where he was welcomed grandly and then sent off in style, as described in *Apache Chronicle*: "Around his arms and legs were fastened gay feathers and jingling bells. He was followed by two Spanish greyhounds, and was accompanied by numerous attractive women who had been given him by the tribes through which he had passed, or whom he took of his own will."

The next phase of Estevanico's journey led him to what is now northwestern New Mexico, to the Zuni River and the city of Hawikuh, near present-day

This 1879 photograph shows the remains of Zuni, one of the pueblos conquered by Coronado. The many ladders gave the inhabitants access to the pueblo's terraced levels.

CORONADO'S EXPEDITION: 1540–1542

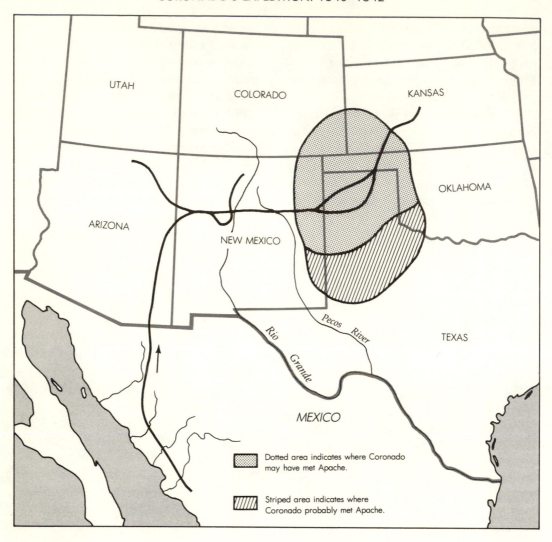

UTAH

COLORADO

KANSAS

OKLAHOMA

ARIZONA

NEW MEXICO

Pecos River

Rio Grande

TEXAS

MEXICO

Dotted area indicates where Coronado
may have met Apache.

Striped area indicates where
Coronado probably met Apache.

Gallup. Hawikuh was a pueblo, a village built of adobe, or clay, houses, and it may have been in existence for 200 years. It was the home of the Zuni, a branch of the Pueblo Indians. Hawikuh was a remarkable place and must have seemed doubly so to an outlander gazing upon it for the first time. But it was not the glittering metropolis envisioned by Mendoza.

The Zuni seized Estevanico and locked him in a hut outside the city. Local leaders interrogated him for three days. Estevanico told them that white men were following close behind him and that they served a powerful lord.

The leaders did not believe him but discerned that the slave represented a foreign people that sought to conquer them. The Zuni killed Estevanico, then diced his body into small pieces, which they distributed among their people as evidence that the strange man was mortal.

Soon after, Friar Marcos, following the trail of his slave, reached Hawikuh. He had learned of Estevanico's gruesome end and did not venture past the outskirts of the pueblo. He claimed the land for the Spanish king and then began the long and arduous journey back to the Spanish settlements of Mexico. He reached Compostela in June 1539 and gave an exaggerated account of his travels to Coronado, who left for Mexico City with the friar. Marcos repeated his fanciful account to Mendoza. He swore Hawikuh was bigger than Mexico City, saying that its surrounding landscape was rich and fertile and that precious minerals abounded—just as Mendoza had hoped. Rumors of the pueblo's riches spread rapidly through the colony. According to Frank Lockwood, author of *Pioneer Days in Arizona*, "Everyone believed his story and everyone took it for granted that these newly discovered cities were rich in minerals and precious stones." At last, it seemed, the seven fabled cities had been found.

Mendoza and Coronado, however, wanted to be sure before mounting an expedition. In September 1539, the viceroy ordered Captain Melchior Díaz, a trustworthy man, to duplicate the journey taken by Friar Marcos. Díaz returned with less encouraging news. He had questioned Indians who knew nothing of gold or other treasures. The friar, hearing of this report, attacked it vehemently and defended his own story so persuasively that Coronado believed him.

On February 23, 1540, Coronado departed from Compostela for Hawikuh with an expeditionary force that included some 250 horsemen, 70 foot soldiers, 300 Mexicans, and 1,000 Indian servants. This cumbersome army plodded across terrain unlike any Friar Marcos had described. It was not green, lush, or inviting but brown, barren, and hostile. Coronado had expected to feed his troops with fruits and vegetables clustered thickly on opulent vines. But nothing edible grew in this sterile desert. Short on food and sapped by the heat, his army sank into exhaustion.

On July 7, 1540, when Coronado drew near Cíbola (the Spanish name for Hawikuh), his men could barely shoulder their weapons. The commander sent peaceful messages to the Indians, who rejected his overtures. Coronado then stormed the pueblo. Weak as his soldiers were, their horses and gunpowder overwhelmed the Zuni, who defended themselves only with arrows, spears, and knives. Hawikuh fell, but Coronado's forces grumbled when they discovered no jewels, no gold, no riches of any kind. They loudly cursed Friar Marcos.

Coronado himself remained convinced, however, that treasures awaited them. He marched on to another pueblo. Again he found no riches. Nor at the next stop. The six cities all resembled Hawikuh: modest places with adobe houses inhabited by people who struggled to gather sufficient food, wove baskets out of desert grasses, and warmed themselves before open campfires built of brushwood. Still, Coronado pushed on. Friar Marcos's fantasy had become his own. He learned of a land to the north called Quivira, besotted with riches. Coronado rode toward it with 30 horsemen.

Once again their hopes were dashed, but Coronado encountered Apache camped at the mouth of the Rio Grande. One of the Spaniards, Pedro de Castañeda, recorded his impressions of the Apache. John Terrell cites them in *The Plains Apache*: "They travel like the Arabs," Castañeda wrote, "with their tents and troops of dogs loaded with poles." The Apache also seemed highly intelligent. "Although they conversed by means of signs they made themselves understood so well there was no need for an interpreter." Coronado himself characterized them as "gentle people, faithful in their friendships." They would not remain so.

At last, in the autumn of 1542, Coronado resigned himself to failure. He led the remnants of his troops back to

Spanish colonists introduced the Apache to firearms. Here warriors use them to guard their wickiup. The two objects in the foreground show that the Apache were far more skilled in basketry than in pottery.

Mexico City and reported to the viceroy. Then he stepped down as governor of Nueva Galicia and retired to the quiet solitude of his Mexican estate.

The Coronado expedition failed, but the hopes that gave rise to it—the dream of riches—continued to inspire Spaniards, and later Americans, as they aggressively and imperiously claimed the lands inhabited by North American Indians. As the 16th-century conquistador Hernán Cortés once told Montezuma, the last of the Aztec rulers of Mexico, "We are troubled with a disease of the heart for which gold is the only remedy." During the next 300 years the gold disease would consume many of those who tried to oust the Apache from their land.

When the first Spanish settlements appeared in the northern provinces of Mexico, the pioneers found the Apache living there to be on peaceful terms with the Pueblo Indians, their neighbors and main trading partners. The Pueblo coveted all the items the Apache produced from slain buffalo—robes, skins, dried meat (or jerky), and more. The Apache willingly exchanged them for the corn, beans, calabash (a gourd whose hollow shell can be used as a vessel), cotton, and various minerals and ceramics available from the Pueblo.

This thriving commerce was disrupted by the Spaniards, who beat the Pueblo into submission and grabbed their goods. Nonetheless, the Apache remained on amicable terms with the Spanish, meeting them at trading posts set up in northern Mexico. The Lipan, Jicarilla, and Mescalero willingly swapped buffalo hides for grain and trinkets. The Apache also picked up other items from the Spanish. One such item was cattle, which the Apache found tasty and nutritious. Another was firearms, Spanish *harquebuses*, or muskets. These large guns lacked the range of the bow and arrow and took much longer to load, but Apache warriors used them effectively to frighten people during raids.

Of much greater value were horses. They afforded Apache warriors tremendous mobility and doubled as pack animals when a group moved camp. Horses also increased Apache contact with other tribes and expanded their opportunities for trade. But what the Apache liked most about horses was their meat. It became a main source of sustenance for them.

But the Spanish were interested in obtaining goods that were not up for barter—Apache slaves—and hunted them ruthlessly. In the process they probably introduced the gruesome practice of scalping, quickly adopted by the Apache, who fought back at every turn. By 1660 a constant state of guerrilla warfare existed between the two peoples. Spanish horsemen terrorized Apache camps, and the Apache frequently set upon the settlers, seizing human captives, horses, cattle, and guns.

In about 1688, the Apache mounted numerous raids on Sonora, a northern

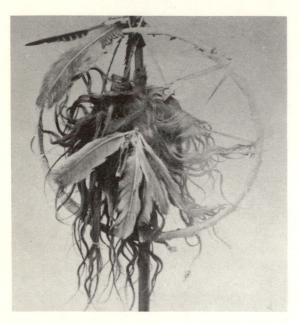

The Spanish probably introduced scalping to Apache culture. In the mid-19th century, the Mexican state of Sonora placed a bounty on the head of every Apache man, woman, and child.

Mexican state bordering Arizona. The Spaniards fought back but were confused by the Apache, whose nomadic habits made them difficult to pin down in pitched battles. The mobility of the Apache enabled them to dictate the time and place of a contest, and the Spaniards worried that they might lose their foothold in northern Mexico. Vicious fighting occurred in the 18th century. Some historians estimate that between 1748 and 1770, the Apache killed 4,000 Spanish settlers and stole or destroyed millions of dollars worth of property.

In 1786, Bernardo de Gálvez, a skilled Indian fighter, became viceroy of Mexico and wrote a treatise, *Instructions for the Governing of the Interior Provinces of New Spain*. Gálvez's treatise drew on some of the warlike policies established by his predecessors, but not all its measures were overtly hostile. For instance, Gálvez urged local colonial authorities to give the Indians gifts, food, and alcohol. He explained that charity would make the Indians dependent on the Spanish, especially when they emptied their flasks. "The supplying of drink to the Indians," Gálvez wrote, "will be a means of gaining their goodwill, discovering their secrets, calming them so they will think less of conceiving and executing their hostilities, and creating for them a new necessity which will oblige them to recognize their dependence upon us more directly." Gálvez also advised that Indians be given faulty muskets so that they would have to rely on the Spanish to repair them.

It is impossible to know how this approach would have fared over time because Gálvez died within months of taking office. He was replaced by Manuel Antonio Flores, who advocated outright extermination of the Indians and beefed up the number of troops sent into their territory. The Apache, defeated in battle, retreated north to Tucson and Tubac (in Arizona). Today the ruins of Tubac's Spanish *presidio*, or fort, still stand, 40 miles south of Tucson on the Santa Cruz River, just north of the Mexican border.

Some Apache fled, but others resumed raiding, angered by the change

In 1786, Bernardo de Gálvez became viceroy of Mexico. He urged colonists to subdue the Apache by giving them alcohol and faulty muskets.

in the Spanish Indian policy after Flores succeeded Gálvez. In 1789 Flores resigned, citing ill health, and yet another viceroy, Conde de Revillagigedo, took over. His policy reverted to the peaceful means promoted by Gálvez. He sought to establish alliances with the Apache and provided them with supplies. It seemed peace had come to *Gran Apacheria* (roughly translated, Great Apache land)—but it proved short lived.

As the 19th century began, the Spanish government abandoned its plan of peaceful coexistence. Furnishing the Apache with clothing, food, and liquor drained community funds. Taxes were introduced, but Spanish colonists objected to paying them. Thus, the Apache saw their supplies dwindle. Those bands camped near the colonists began to drift away, joining forces with those who had never yielded to the

This southwestern presidio—or fort—*housed Mexican troops who frequently clashed with Apache in the 18th and 19th centuries.*

Spaniards' offer of friendship. Soon butchery resumed—on both sides.

The Spanish continued to take a peaceful approach to the Apache on only one front: religion. From the outset of their colonial adventures in the New World, the Spaniards had tried to wean native peoples away from their own religion and toward Roman Catholicism. Church missionaries, such as Friar Marcos, traveled with conquistadores. As the conquerors subdued Indians by force, holy men tried to guide them peaceably into the Christian faith by "educating" them at missionary churches staffed by clergy. Sometimes missionaries were the first white men ever glimpsed by Indians. This was so especially in the southeastern areas of North America, in present-day Florida and Georgia, where by the early 1600s there may have been 40 different missions supervising the lives of 20,000 Indians, all of whom converted to Christianity.

To these religious emissaries, the Apache religion—their gods, legends, and rituals—seemed crude and barbaric. The Apache, in turn, viewed Christianity as alien. Christians worshiped inside buildings and fixed their attention on a raised altar that depicted the suffering body of Christ. The Apache conducted their ceremonies outdoors and lifted their gaze toward the limitless vault of the sky.

Nonetheless, many Apache were converted from their own religion to Roman Catholicism, though not always

with the results hoped for by missionaries. In fact, one convert became a scourge to the very people who took him under their wing. His name was Juan José, and he lived in the early 19th century. Juan José was born a Mimbres Apache of the Eastern Chiricahua band. At an early age he was packed off by Spanish authorities to a mission school, one of the numerous places where Roman Catholicism was taught to Indian children. Juan José had an aptitude for learning and was encouraged by his teachers to study for the priesthood. He heeded their advice and dedicated himself to Christianity—until 1835, when he discovered that his father had been murdered by Mexicans.

Juan José abruptly quit the mission and returned to his band, anxious for revenge. He rose to a high position and led a group of warriors who mounted vicious attacks on Mexican settlements. Because Juan José had been exposed to the ways of the settlers he knew how best to weaken them. He robbed their mail and captured messengers, forcing them to divulge crucial information.

Even as he wreaked havoc among the colonists, Juan José stayed on friendly terms with a trader in Sonora, Mexico—an American named James Johnson who bought Juan José's stolen goods. Their relationship was on solid footing when the Apache intercepted a letter to Johnson sent by the Mexican government, which offered the trader a handsome reward for Juan José's scalp. Juan José confronted Johnson

Missionaries converted many American Indians to Roman Catholicism, but most Apache found the religion at odds with their own practices.

with this evidence, but the American convinced him of his loyalty and then accepted an invitation to the Apache's camp. Johnson arrived laden with gifts. He heaped them in a pile that contained a hidden fuse. As the Apache crowded around, Johnson secretly tossed a match, igniting a howitzer (a small cannon). It spat out lead projectiles that killed many Apache and wounded oth-

ers, including Juan José, who struggled with one of Johnson's American companions. Johnson then shot José in the back, killing him and betraying their friendship.

The Apache were embittered by other, similar episodes. One of them occurred in the summer of 1850. At that time many Warm Springs Apache—of the Eastern Chiricahua band—camped along the San Miguel River near Ramos, about 80 miles south of Columbus, New Mexico. The band traded in town during the day, and at night they sang, danced, and gambled in their camp.

One day local Mexicans invited the Apache into Ramos to join them in drinking mescal, a type of liquor distilled from spiny leaves of maguey plants. The Mexicans furnished an unlimited supply of the alcohol free of charge, and many of the Indians became intoxicated. They returned to the camp and fell into a drunken sleep. Then, before dawn, the Mexican villagers crept into the Apache camp and began killing the sleeping Indians. Jason Betzinger and W. S. Nye describe the scene in *I Fought with Geronimo*: "There were curses in Spanish, thuds, grunts, a few screams, and the whimpering of a child. Here and there a rustle

When the United States expanded its borders into the Southwest, traders dealt with Apache at posts like this one in Ganado, Arizona.

Miguel Hidalgo y Costilla, a priest, led Mexico's uprising against Spain in 1810 and was executed by royalist forces in 1811.

of Sonora put a bounty on the head of all Apache men, women, and children. It was difficult, however, to distinguish an Apache scalp from any other. John Terrell writes in *Apache Chronicle* that "on several occasions bounty hunters wiped out Mexican villages, scalped their victims, young and old, male and female, and delivered the scalps to the authorities for payment with the claim that they had been taken from Apaches."

One reason the situation became so violent was that Mexico was trying to consolidate its power as part of its struggle for independence from Spain. As early as 1810, Mexican colonials led by Hidalgo y Costilla, a priest, had rebelled against the mother country. During the next decade, Mexican insurrectionists battled troops loyal to Spain, and in 1821, Spain accepted Mexico's independence as a European-style monarchy. Two years later, a republic was set up, but the government was run by self-serving individuals who vied for power and wealth. Mexico suffered a succession of leaders, none able to cure its economic and social ills.

The problems intensified in 1846, when Mexico went to war with the United States over Texas, which at the time belonged to Mexico but wanted to become an independent republic. The fighting lasted two years and ended with Mexico's surrender to the United States in 1848. The Treaty of Guadalupe-Hidalgo granted independence to Texas and ceded to the United States a

told where some more alert Indian managed to steal away in the semi-darkness. But there were few such. In a short time most of the Indians were lying in their blood, dead or dying."

Throughout this period Spanish-Mexican officials formally kept up peaceful relations with the Apache. Viceroys monkeyed with strategies, some favoring war, others peace. But in reality confusion reigned. The state vast territory that included the northern parts of New Mexico and Arizona. Five years later the southern parts of these states went to the United States as part of the Gadsden Purchase, a $10 million sale that enabled the American government to route a southern railroad through areas inhabited by Indians.

The 1848 treaty included a provision that had important consequences for the Apache. The United States agreed to prevent Indians residing in its newly acquired lands from going south to raid settlements in Mexico. If such raids occurred, the United States agreed to punish those responsible and to stop its own citizens from purchasing goods or livestock brought back over the border. The Americans also agreed to compensate Mexicans for any losses they sustained. This provision pitted the United States against the Apache, for whom raiding had become habit. A new enemy of the Indian had emerged. ▲

AN ACCOUNT OF

CALIFORNIA,

AND THE

WONDERFUL GOLD REGIONS.

A New Arrival at the Gold Diggings.

WITH A DESCRIPTION OF

The Different Routes to California;

Information about the Country, and the Ancient and Modern Discoveries of Gold;

How to Test Precious Metals; Accounts of Gold Hunters;

TOGETHER WITH MUCH OTHER

Useful Reading for those going to California, or having Friends there.

ILLUSTRATED WITH MAPS AND ENGRAVINGS.

BOSTON:
PUBLISHED BY J. B. HALL, 66 CORNHILL.
For Sale at Skinner's Publication Rooms, 60½ Cornhill.

Price, 12½ cents.

The 1849 gold rush brought a stream of prospectors into the Southwest and began a new chapter of Apache history.

THE
AMERICANS

At the time Texas was agitating for liberation from Mexico it had a large population of English-speaking Americans. By 1834, 20,000 settlers had moved to the settlement of Austin and outnumbered Mexicans in the region 4 to 1. After the United States won the Mexican War, a general westward expansion began as people living in the established states on the eastern seaboard yearned for land and space.

In 1848, gold was discovered in California. Over the next two years thousands of American and European prospectors streamed across the continent in search of the precious ore. In the 1850s, the pioneer spirit took hold. Railroads enabled farmers in the Midwest—Illinois, Iowa, Minnesota, and neighboring states—to transport goods back east. The 1860s and 70s saw an influx of farmers from Germany and Scandinavia who trekked to western territories that, as a result of the 1862 Homestead Act, offered 160 acres practically free to anyone willing to cultivate them.

By the mid-19th century, more than 200,000 Indians inhabited the Great Plains and the Rocky Mountains. But they faced the arrival of American miners, railroads, and cattlemen, all assisted by the United States government, which had declared a policy of Manifest Destiny meant to expand the nation's borders to California and the Pacific Ocean. The Indians, separated into distinct nations that were subdivided further into tribes, bands, and local groups, struggled to hold back the tide.

The Apache proved especially fierce in the defense of their land and way of life. They came into conflict with the United States soon after it acquired Texas (which was granted statehood in 1845) and the vast territory ceded by Mexico. Of a total population of about 100,000, there were 60,000 Mexicans. The rest were Indians, 6,000 to 8,000 of them Apache. This tiny number had little chance of fending off the U.S. Army, which governed the area.

At first the Apache fought the troops, but then, in 1850, leaders of the Mescalero in New Mexico's Sierra Blancas informed the American military that they would exchange all their captives and stolen property and sign a treaty.

The 1862 Homestead Act granted large tracts of land to Americans and Europeans willing to clear and cultivate the acreage themselves.

The Mescalero chiefs called a meeting with the Jicarilla and Comanche. The various bands stopped raiding and awaited developments. The Americans, who had only 1,300 soldiers, agreed to end hostilities. In 1851, James S. Calhoun—governor of the New Mexico territory and its superintendent of Indian Affairs—signed a treaty with the Jicarilla and with two Mescalero leaders, Lobo and Josécito. An enlightened man, Calhoun sought to extend the pact. He planned to visit another Apache band, the Eastern Chiricahua, who were camped at Santa Rita.

But Calhoun's good intentions met with resistance from the U.S. Army. A change of command put a new officer in charge of the Ninth Military Department, which supervised affairs in New Mexico. He was Edwin Vose Sumner, who in 1851 arrived in New Mexico and completely altered the strategy there. He removed troops from the towns where they had been posted and stationed them at forts situated in key places. The soldiers were ordered to build these posts themselves, and many sprang up, including Ft. Webster, erected in Apache territory.

At the same time that Sumner initiated this new strategy, he was expected to cooperate with Calhoun, who still occupied the post of governor and superintendent. But Sumner took his first responsibility—to quell any Indian threat—more seriously than his second. He halted Calhoun's attempt to make peace with the Warm Springs Apache of the Eastern Chiricahua band.

The Warm Springs Apache were known in their own language as the *Tci-he-ende*, or "Red-paint People," after the color of their war paint, a broad clay stripe across the face. Their leader, Mangas Coloradas (Spanish for Red Sleeves), the successor to Juan José, was the most imposing Apache chief of his time. A physical giant who was also intelligent and shrewd, he behaved in the classic manner of the Apache leader. So respected was he that his following reached beyond his own band.

Mangas had little respect for whites, or *pindah-lickoyee* (white-eyed enemies), and his contempt for them grew when prospectors working the mines at Santa Rita killed Apache without provocation and without being punished by the American government. Yet Mangas dealt with the whites on their terms. Instead of avenging the murder of his people, he insisted only that those re-

sponsible be tried for the crime. Mangas changed his approach, however, when a new gold-mining site was built at a nearby spot, Piños Altos. The chief visited the miners and asked them to leave, recommending that they move south of the border to Sonora, which had richer deposits of ore. Suspecting a ruse, the miners tied the chief to a post, whipped him mercilessly, and then taunted him as he staggered away.

Mangas got his revenge. In February 1852 he began a rampage that the Americans could not stop. The Apache raided mail carriages and murdered those aboard, plundered a federal wagon train (only the drivers escaped), and killed soldiers sent to capture them. American troops did not catch Mangas until 1863, when he was in his sixties, and then only by deception. A group of 40 prospectors traveling through Apache territory decided to kidnap Mangas in order to forestall conflict with his band. They persuaded a military unit to back them and then asked Mangas to appear at their camp to discuss terms for peace. Mangas arrived and was whisked away to a military camp. He was interrogated, tortured, and shot. The soldiers then scalped him and sent his skull to a phrenologist (a person who analyzes one's character by studying the shape of the subject's skull; phrenology is a pseudoscience that was popular in Europe and America in the 19th century).

Thievery, murder, and massacre—conducted by both Americans and the

Apache—plunged the Southwest into another violent phase. Sometimes safety could be found only in the old forts of Tucson and Tubac. In 1850, the Apache attacked Tucson. According to *Victorio and the Mimbres Apaches*, by historian Dan Thrapp, "Anything went, provided one could seize the advantage. Even such servants of mercy as physicians were not above falling into line. One doctor, called upon to treat an Apache whose leg had been punctured by a bullet, unnecessarily amputated the limb at the hip. . . since he believed him to be . . . [a frequent] raider."

Captain John Bourke described the effects of an Apache attack on a wagon train:

It was a ghastly sight. . . . There were the hot embers of the new wagons, the scattered fragments of broken boxes, barrels and packages of all sorts, broken rifles, torn and burned clothing. There lay all that was mortal of poor [pioneer Newton] Israel, stripped of clothing, a small piece cut from the crown of the head, but thrown back upon the corpse—the Apache do not care much for scalping—his heart cut out, but also thrown back near the corpse, which had been dragged to the fire of the burning wagons and had been partly consumed; a lance wound in the back, one or two arrow wounds . . . a severe contusion under the left eye, where he had been hit, perhaps with the stock of a rifle or carbine, and the death wound from ear to ear.

The acquisition of territory from Mexico enabled the United States to route the transcontinental railroad through Apache land.

Apache often raided wagon trains such as this ox-drawn caravan transporting supplies to the Union Pacific Railroad in the 1860s.

Another violent incident occurred in the winter of 1863–64 and involved the Pinal and Coyotero bands, both subdivisions of the Western Apache. Indians had stolen livestock from settlers living near Peeple Valley in Yavapai County, about 20 miles southwest of Prescott, Arizona. In January 1864, King Woolsey, an aide to the territorial governor of Arizona—it was not yet a state—led a group of settlers against the raiders. His terse report of the conflict, quoted by Frank Lockwood in *Apache Indians*, published in 1938, described the incident in this way: "On January 24, 1864, a party of thirty Americans and fourteen Maricopa and Pima Indians . . . attacked a band of Gila Apaches and killed nineteen of them and wounded others. Mr. Cyrus Lennon

Wolsey's party was killed by a wounded Indian.''

In truth, the battle was more complicated, at least to judge from stories circulated by Arizona pioneers. According to them, the Apache trapped Woolsey and his party in the Tonto Basin, south of Payson in Gila County. The Apache held the high ground above the pioneers, who called a truce. Through an interpreter Woolsey called a council with about 30 of the Indian warriors. Before going off to meet them, he instructed a rear guard of some 200 men to open fire when he touched his hat. Woolsey then set off with three other men, each carrying a concealed revolver. They met with the Apache warriors, who had hidden weapons of their own—knives. After the meeting began, a young Apache boy arrived with the news that their leader wanted his warriors to return in order to help kill the whites and their Indian allies. At this point Woolsey touched his hat and his men loosed their fire.

Yet another grim episode, known as the Camp Grant Massacre, occurred on April 30, 1871. The preceding February, 150 Aravaipa, another Western Apache band, sought refuge at Camp Grant, located about 60 miles northeast of Tucson, Arizona. These Apache feared American troops and had taken to living in the mountains, where freezing temperatures and a poor food supply had caused many in the group to die. They hoped to return to their former home near Aravaipa Creek, where they could plant crops and live more comfortably. This home happened to be in the vicinity of Camp Grant, and the Apache appeared there one day and asked for permission to live nearby, under the protection of the troops.

The garrison's ranking officer, Lieutenant Royal Emerson Whitman, invited the Apache to stay on the premises while he awaited approval from his superiors in California. Whitman provided the Apache with rations and let them gather food in the surrounding area. He also employed them as hay gatherers for the garrison's horses, paying them a penny per pound. Soon the number of Apache grew to 500 as word spread among groups that Lieutenant Whitman could be counted on for assistance and protection. In April a new commander, Captain Frank Stanwood, arrived at the fort. Whitman explained the unusual arrangement, and Stanwood approved it. Two weeks later, word finally came from California, but it was useless: Whitman's letter did not conform exactly to army regulations, so the general had declined to answer it, a convenient way to ignore the issue.

Nonetheless, the arrangement continued. Later in April, Captain Stanwood left camp on a long scouting mission, taking most of the troops with him. Whitman stayed behind with about 50 soldiers. Stanwood had not yet returned on April 30, when a messenger appeared at Camp Grant and informed him that a civilian posse from

A painting by Frederic Remington shows Chiricahua returning to their mountain retreat after a raid. The warriors probably divided the booty among the band.

Tucson, which had suffered repeated Apache raids, was riding toward Camp Grant. Whitman immediately sent interpreters to warn the Indians and direct them to shelter inside the fort.

It was too late. A mob of 148 civilians—6 whites, 48 Mexicans, and 94 Papago Indians (another southwestern people)—with ammunition and provisions furnished by the adjutant general of Arizona Territory, set upon the sleeping Apache. The Indians had no weapons. Worse yet, the men in the camp had gone hunting in the mountains, leaving the women and children defenseless. One hundred people were shot or clubbed to death. Twenty-nine children survived, and the vigilantes took them as captives. Two escaped; 5 ended up in the hands of Arizona citizens, who turned them over to the government; the remaining 22 were sold into slavery in Mexico. American newspapers gloried in the bloodshed. The *Denver News* crowed: "We give this act of the citizens of Arizona most hearty and unqualified endorsement. We congratulate them on the fact that permanent peace arrangements have been made with so many, and we regret that the number was not double."

The president of the United States, Ulysses S. Grant (1869–77), was horrified by the incident and demanded that the vigilantes be tried. Charges were brought against 104 people, and the jury deliberated for 20 minutes before finding them all innocent.

Desolation, destruction, and death seemed the bywords of the new territories. An article written in 1910 in Texas's *El Paso Morning Times* summarized the feeling of most Americans: "The only means of persuasion at the time with an Apache was by means of a Winchester with a cool head and a clear eye at the other end."

As that comment indicates, Texas had a history of treating the Apache badly. In 1855 two small reserves were set aside in the northern area of the state for its population of Mescalero, and there was talk of granting the band more land. Yet in 1859, before any reservation could be established, vigilantes raided the already existing reserves, and concerned officials quickly sent Indians to protected territory in Oklahoma. After the demise of the Texas reservations, Texans considered the remaining Mescalero fair game. When Major Robert Neighbors, the U.S. superintendent of Indian Affairs for Texas, tried to protect the band and its property, he was assassinated.

New Mexico proved equally hostile to the Mescalero living there. The territory grew in population as new lands were opened by the U.S. government after the discovery of gold in 1848 in nearby Colorado and California and fol-

The U.S. government erected forts throughout Apache territory. Charles Schreyvogel's Defending the Stockade *shows troops fending off a surprise attack.*

lowing the Mexican War and the Gadsden Purchase. Prospectors poured into the area, and settlers occupied land that had traditionally belonged to the Mescalero. These newcomers also killed buffalo and other game prized by the Apache. Worse, they did it for sport rather than for sustenance.

The Mescalero attacked the settlers, hoping to drive them off the land. The American military responded in kind. Forts arose throughout the Mescalero area, and conflict raged on. During the Civil War (1861–65), some Union troops were stationed in the Southwest. One of their commanders, General James H. Carleton, who had fought the Jicarilla in 1854, decided to clear up the problem. In 1862, he ordered some of his men to build a post in east-central New Mexico—Ft. Sumner—near a place called Bosque Redondo (Spanish for Round Grove) on the Pecos River, where some cottonwoods grew. There, on an area of about 40 square miles, Carleton intended to create a reservation. All the local Indians were ordered to appear there. A total of 9,000 Navajo and 500 Mescalero complied in order to escape murder at the hands of Carleton's forces.

The area could not support so large a population, however, and by 1864 the Mescalero and Navajo had begun squabbling. Most of the Mescalero escaped and made their way back to their traditional lands. In 1866, U.S. Army authorities relieved Carleton of his command, and the government concluded that the Bosque was unsuitable for a reservation.

In 1872, the federal government attempted to establish a separate reservation for the Mescalero. The next year, an executive order issued by President Grant established reservations on the eastern slopes of the White and Sacramento mountains, located in south-central New Mexico, east of the Rio Grande. Any Mescalero found outside these designated areas would be treated as hostile by the military. In 1880, the government ordered the band to Ft. Stanton, also in south-central New Mexico. When they arrived, they were stripped of their weapons and horses. Fourteen Mescalero resisted. The soldiers killed them. Others fled. Those who submitted to the troops were held in a corral filled with manure. Some Apache grew ill, and the authorities were compelled to release them with the stipulation that they remain near the fort. Later that year they moved into a reservation.

The troubles between the Jicarilla and the United States began after the United States acquired New Mexico. In October 1849, Jicarilla warriors joined those from another Indian nation, the Ute, in an attack on American troops at the Cimarron River cutoff of the Santa Fe Trail. The next month they struck the trail again, raiding an eastbound mail party. American forces retaliated, and a pattern began that lasted through the year. In 1850, the U.S. Army built forts in Jicarilla territory.

The next year, the band signed a treaty with the U.S. government. They agreed to stop raiding settlements, to return what they had stolen, to live by farming, and to accept confinement within a reservation. In return the government offered them financial aid. The treaty failed, however, to win approval from the U.S. Congress, and the Jicarilla received no assistance from the government. They nevertheless abided by the unratified agreement and staged only a few raids.

In 1852, William Lane, the territorial governor, began settling the band on land west of the Rio Grande on the Rio Puerco. He was acting on his own—the federal government had not authorized such a reservation. One Jicarilla band cleared more than a hundred acres and planted crops, eliminating their need to raid. Lane seemed to have hit upon the ideal solution for lessening hostilities, but he was ordered to suspend his program by the federal government in Washington, D.C.

As a result the Jicarilla resumed raiding in order to feed themselves. In 1854, the acting governor of New Mexico declared war on the band. He sent an army after them, and it pursued the Jicarilla throughout northern New Mexico and southern Colorado. Eventually, both sides agreed to negotiate and signed another peace treaty in September 1855. But again, approval failed to come from Congress, which remained skeptical. The Jicarilla continued to live in the area and supported themselves by hunting, farming, and gathering.

From 1855 to 1887, the government mulled over various plans for coming to terms with the Jicarilla, who by 1873 were the only tribe in New Mexico not living on a reservation. A favored solution was to settle the Jicarilla on reservations alongside other Indians. But this never worked. In 1873, the parties signed yet a third treaty. It granted the band a reservation in northwest New Mexico. White settlers demanded this land, however, and in 1876 the territorial government refused to abide by the treaty's provisions.

Four years later, the government established another reservation for the Jicarilla in north-central New Mexico. Again, the program failed, and the band was sent to the Mescalero reservation. In 1887, the government reestablished the reservation opened in 1880, and the Jicarilla finally came into land of their own.

The Western Apache lived in east-central Arizona. After the United States acquired that territory as part of the Gadsden Purchase, conflicts arose. As was the case with the other Apache, settlers and miners encroached on their land. Hostilities erupted and lasted some 40 years. In 1864, the United States established Camp Goodwin on the Gila River in White Mountain Apache territory. The fort isolated the White Mountain and Cibecue Apache. These Western bands—mindful of the fate that befell other Apache—quickly made peace with the United States government. They continued to raid Mexican villages, however.

By the late 19th century, it was clear to the Apache that the American government intended to pin them on the margins of the growing republic. Following the Camp Grant Massacre, the government initiated a new peace policy designed to gather all the Apache on reservations. The plan called for each of the Apache bands to be given its own land, where they could live unmolested by white miners and settlers and where they could be taught to farm, so that raiding would no longer be necessary.

In 1871–72, the federal government established four Apache reservations. The Cibecue and the northern bands of the White Mountain Apache were given the area around Ft. Apache, in east-central Arizona. Camp Verde, northeast of Phoenix, Arizona, went to the Northern and Southern Tonto and some of the Yavapai. The San Carlos Apache and the Southern White Mountain groups moved to San Carlos, in southeastern Arizona. And the Chiricahua were granted a reservation in Cochise County of southeastern Arizona.

General George Crook, the renowned Indian fighter, flanked by two Apache scouts, Dulchy (left) and Alchise. Crook admired the skill and stamina of Apache warriors and hired them to help his own troops in the 1870s.

Apache warriors adapted their ancestral customs to the demands of modern warfare. Here riflemen employed by the U.S. Army wear ammunition belts over their breechcloths.

At first it seemed this policy might eliminate warfare between the Apache and the United States. In 1872, General George Crook, a longtime Indian fighter celebrated for his conquest of the Paiute nation, was placed in command of the Arizona Department, following the Camp Grant Massacre. Crook sympathized with the Apache plight and generally treated them fairly. He knew that they fought because they had to. "The American Indian commands respect," he once remarked, "only as long as he inspires terror with his rifle."

Crook's appointed task, however, was to subdue the Apache, and he set about doing this with all the fervor of a dedicated military man. He had some novel ideas about how best to fight the Apache. He abandoned wagon trains for pack mules that could negotiate the mountainous terrain where the Apache liked to conduct warfare. And Crook thought that American soldiers, unused to the rigors of the desert, were no match for Apache warriors, with their remarkable stamina and durability. Thus, he favored winning over friendly Apache to act as scouts and fighters in his own army. Crook's approach met with disapproval from Americans who balked at the prospect of fighting side by side with Indians.

As Apache raids continued, Crook began a campaign to scoop up all the Apache not settled on reservations. In 1872 he moved against the Tonto band and defeated them in a few months. Then, in 1874, American policy shifted once more, this time toward "concentration." This policy dictated that three Apache bands—the Western, Chiricahua, and Yavapai—be placed on one reservation, San Carlos, where they could be managed more easily. In 1875 the government began gathering the Apache. It was a flawed idea. Forcing different bands to live together caused hostility and suspicion among them. Factions arose. Some groups wanted war, others peace, still others to escape. Many did flee, and General Crook was ordered to track them down, especially those Chiricahua who had broken away and mounted several raids.

Perhaps the most tenacious of all the Apache bands was the Chiricahua, who launched a 25-year war against the United States in northern Mexico, Arizona, and New Mexico. The battle began in October 1860, when Apache from an unidentified band raided a ranch owned by the Wards, homesteaders near Tubac, Arizona. The band spirited away livestock and the Wards' 12-year-old son, Felix. His father, John Ward, followed the raiders' trail and became convinced they were Chiricahua led by the renowned warrior Cochise.

Ward reported his beliefs to the commanding officer at Ft. Buchanan, and in January 1860 about 50 soldiers were sent to Apache Pass in southeastern Arizona. Their newly commissioned second lieutenant, George Bascom, was ordered to recover the boy and the cattle, by force if necessary.

After reaching the pass, Bascom's company camped in Siphon Canyon, about a mile from Ft. Bowie near a stagecoach station. Cochise appeared with an escort of warriors, one carrying a white flag. Bascom and Cochise exchanged polite greetings. Then the Apache entered Bascom's tent. Bascom accused Cochise of stealing the livestock and kidnapping the boy. Cochise denied having any knowledge of the incident and offered to help obtain information and to recover the boy. Bascom then called Cochise a liar and told him that he and his warriors would be imprisoned if Felix Ward and the stolen cattle were not returned.

The lieutenant had anticipated trouble with Cochise and had previously ordered soldiers to surround the tent. They now closed in. Cochise suddenly pulled out his knife and slit open the wall to Bascom's tent. He climbed through it and escaped the camp, eluding gunfire. His six warriors remained in Bascom's custody, however. The next day Cochise returned to the stagecoach station with a chief of the Coyotero band and 500 warriors. Cochise took the stationmaster captive and killed two other employees who tried to escape.

That night Cochise attacked the eastbound Overland Mail Coach and a small wagon train. He brutally killed all the teamsters—or drivers—but three, whom he took captive. Occasional fighting continued during the next several days. Cochise held the upper hand over Bascom and his small company. Then two columns of American soldiers arrived at Apache Pass, and the Chiricahua retreated into the surrounding hills. On February 18, the combined American military forces marched out of the pass. The troops observed a flock of buzzards circling overhead. Officers sent advance scouts to investigate. They discovered the corpses of Cochise's captives.

The senior American officer, Captain Irwin, who had arrived at the head of one of the relief columns, ordered the execution of the Apache still in his custody. Three of them were related by blood to Cochise. Within 60 days, the Chiricahua killed 150 white people, and for years no traveler found safety along the Overland Trail.

Cochise had not been lying to Bascom. It was a band of Pinal, Western Apache, who had raided the Ward ranch. Had Bascom been more experienced he would not have doubted the chief's word. Seasoned soldiers and government officials had learned to trust Cochise and to hold him in high regard. And indeed he was one of the premier Indian leaders of his era. The son-in-law of Mangas Coloradas, Cochise had won a loyal following by the time of the Chiricahua Wars. He was then in his late thirties, an average-sized man who excelled in combat as a strategist and fighter. He was also a skilled raider who provided amply for his band and could be counted on for guidance and sympathy.

Apache recruited by the U.S Army gather outside the guardhouse of the San Carlos Reservation in 1880, four years after the Chiricahua were forced to live there alongside Western Apache.

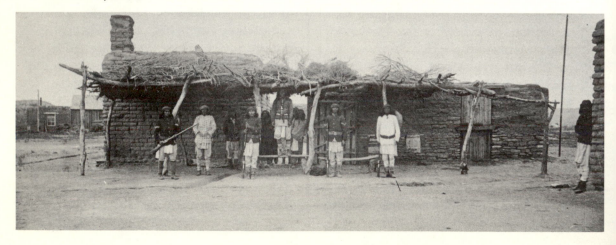

This photograph of children in Geronimo's camp at Skeleton Canyon—on the border of New Mexico and Mexico— was taken in 1886, shortly before he surrendered to the U.S. government.

In 1872, Cochise agreed to a peace treaty that gave the Chiricahua a reservation on their homeland in southeastern Arizona. Two years later, Cochise died. In 1875 the Bureau of Indian Affairs (BIA) reported that raids in the area had ceased. But the bureau's policy of concentration shattered this long-awaited calm. The Chiricahua objected to being removed from their homeland to the San Carlos Agency, a reservation in south-central Arizona. The band disliked both the land and the agency. As one Apache told Eve Ball, author of *In the Days of Victorio*: "Take stones and ashes and thorns, with some scorpions and rattlesnakes thrown in, dump the outfit on stones, heat the stones red hot, set the United States Army after the Apache, and you have San Carlos." The Chiricahua also regarded the other Apache at San Carlos with hostility and suspicion. Even so, in 1876 the government abolished the Chiricahua reservation and moved 322 people—mainly women, children, and old men—to the new place. The remainder fled to the Warm Springs reservation, to the mountains, or to Mexico.

Two years later, a band led by Geronimo, another brilliant Chiricahua chief, raided American settlements in southern Arizona and New Mexico. He was captured quickly and sent to San Carlos, but he eventually escaped. That

(continued on page 90)

GERONIMO, THE LAST WARRIOR

Geronimo was born in the early 1820s in the area that is now southwestern Arizona. Not until he was nearly 80 years old did the short and muscular warrior surrender to U.S. Army forces at Skeleton Canyon, on the border of New Mexico and Mexico, approximately 100 miles away form his birthplace. Geronimo was the last Apache leader to resist capture by army forces. In fact, he never was captured but voluntarily led his rebel Chiricahua band to surrender in 1886 to end the era of the Apache wars in the American Southwest.

Geronimo had submitted to captivity on an Arizona reservation twice before but each time changed his mind and escaped to Mexico, where he hid with other Indians in the Sierra Madre. Along the way, Geronimo raided Mexican and American villages, stole horses and cattle, and murdered

Geronimo (at the wheel) goes for a spin on the Ft. Sill Reservation in 1908, a year before his death.

innocent people. He was accused of even more violence and savagery by army officials and the American public. Eventually, Geronimo came to symbolize Indian ferocity. After his final surrender, he was known as "the Apache terror."

One army aide, Britton Davis, who was in charge of leading the Indian scouts who searched for Geronimo's hideouts, described the warrior as "a thoroughly vicious . . . and treacherous man. His only redeeming traits were courage and determinism. His word, no matter how earnestly pledged, was worthless." But Geronimo claimed otherwise. "I never do wrong without a cause," he declared. "Several times I have asked for peace, but trouble has come from the agents and interpreters."

Despite his skillful leadership in battle, Geronimo never held the post of war chief. He was instead a *di-yin*, or shaman, who gained others' respect and awe by using powers he believed were granted to him by supernatural spirits. In wartime, Geronimo relied on his clairvoyance and called on spirits to help him discover enemy camps, pray for victory, and make war charms that brought protection and good luck. One follower credited Geronimo with having once stopped the sun and extended night for two hours so that the war party could approach the enemy in the dark.

In 1895, after Geronimo's final surrender and relocation to Ft. Sill, Oklahoma, he no longer summoned his supernatural powers. He turned instead to other survival instincts that allowed him to prosper in captivity even as many of his compatriots struggled and died. Gifted with a keen business sense, Geronimo sold tourists autographs, photographs, and buttons from his coat. Painters paid him to sit for portraits, and exhibitors paid him to appear in Indian shows. In 1905, he received $171 to ride in costume on horseback in President Theodore Roosevelt's inaugural parade as proof of the government's intention to "civilize" Indians. In the same year, Geronimo began dictating his own version of his transformation from free Apache to prisoner of war. S. M. Barrett, a school superintendent, wrote down the account, which was published in 1907 as *Geronimo's Story of His Life*.

In 1909, at about the age of 80, Geronimo got drunk one night at Ft. Sill. He fell off of his horse and into a creek, where he lay until the next morning. He did not drown, but he developed pneumonia and soon died.

(continued from page 87)

year the government also subjected the Warm Springs band to the concentration policy, but only 450 out of a total population of 2,000 could be rounded up for removal. The rest formed raiding groups led by Chief Victorio. A tragic and unbreakable cycle of Apache behavior had emerged—one of surrender, escape, and raid, repeated until the band had exhausted its numbers and strength.

In October 1880, Mexicans destroyed Victorio's raiding band at Tres Castillos in northern Mexico. Of the Warm Springs Apache, only the leader Naña and his followers remained on the loose. At long last, on September 4, 1886, Geronimo finally surrendered. Peace had come to Gran Apacheria. The government decided to rid itself of the Chiricahua problem by classifying all its living members as prisoners of war and

In 1886, the U.S. government exiled Chiricahua to distant states. In this photograph, a band headed for Florida rests at a stop near Nueces River, Texas.

The Ft. Sill Reservation, Oklahoma, in 1871, when it was inhabited mainly by Kiowa and Comanche. Later, Mangas Coloradas and Geronimo both died there.

exiling them, first to Florida, then to Alabama, and finally to Oklahoma.

Geronimo went into exile, along with his followers and 382 others, including some of the U.S. Army's own Apache scouts. Most of the band's graves are located at Ft. Sill, Oklahoma. As the artillery thunders on a nearby test range, one can stand amid their remains. Geronimo's grave was desecrated long ago by vandals, who toppled the stone eagle that marked his burial site. An artillery barrage sounds a funeral dirge, perhaps to remind tourists of the U.S. Army's victory, perhaps to assure the government that the proud Chiricahua have indeed succumbed. ▲

The Lipan schoolgirl (middle, second row) in this photograph, taken in about 1900, was one of the few survivors of her band.

RESERVATION LIFE

By 1890 all the Apache bands had submitted to the U.S. government's reservation policy, which recognized them as distinct subgroups functioning outside the mainstream of American society. The Apache were not entirely free of the government, however. The BIA vowed to turn reservations into "schools for civilization." By this time the total American-Indian population had been reduced to about 300,000, less than one-third of what it had been when Columbus first landed in the New World.

Although reservations were meant to recognize the separateness of America's Indian population, they served mainly to transfer control over Indian life from the U.S. Army to the BIA, which supervised law enforcement, education, health, and land development. In 1878 the BIA set up a police force that had almost unlimited power to prosecute and punish Indians. Within 6 years, the U.S. Indian Police—all white men—operated in 48 of the 60 reservations.

The key white figure on each reservation was the agent, a government official who assumed the task of "civilizing" Indians. In general that meant converting Indians to Christianity and instructing them in farming. Tilling the soil brought unwelcome changes to age-old Indian cultures. Jacob Dunn voiced a commonly held view when he asserted in *Massacres of the Mountains*, published in 1886, that the typical Apache warrior could not "feel that fighting is the only work that a man ought to do, and then take kindly to ploughing. His spirit must be broken in some way, or his nature changed, before he will submit to it. The right or wrong of breaking his spirit is another question; the fact remains that he must be born again in civilization."

"Born again" was another phrase, like "schools for civilization," that sounded loftier than its actual purpose proved. For in the early years of the reservations, the true aim of the government was the systematic destruction of the Apache way of life, which was

93

This photo dates from 1905, when Apache on the Mescalero reservation in New Mexico chose to live in tipis situated hundreds of yards away from agency buildings.

to be replaced with, in the ringing tones of one noted Indian agent, Dr. Michael Steck, a "laudable desire to accumulate and retain property." Thus, agents discouraged traditional Apache ceremonies, such as the healing rituals, that involved giving away material goods. And the Indian Police functioned, on the whole, as a means to strip power away from traditional group and band leaders. When the Apache resisted, agents often threatened to reduce their food rations. In fact the threat of starvation became the preferred method of

"civilizing" Indians. After a century of effort, the U.S. government's twin project—guiding the Apache toward both Christianity and farming—has met with mixed success. Many have become Christians, yet shamans still are sought out as healers. All Apache learn English, but most prefer to use their native language. And ceremonies, such as the girls' puberty rite, are still practiced by many Apache.

Gradually, the government has come to recognize that Indians are proud of their heritage and want to preserve it—without being denied the opportunities given other Americans. In March 1968, President Lyndon B. Johnson (1963–69) sent a message on Indian affairs to Congress. He proposed to "erase old attitudes of paternalism" and "to promote partnership and self-help." He added, "Our goal must be: A standard of living for Indians equal to that of the country as a whole, freedom of choice—and opportunity to remain in their homeland, if they choose, without surrendering their dignity, and an opportunity to move to the towns and cities of America if they choose,

equipped with skills to live in equality and dignity; full participation in the life of modern America, with a full share of economic and social justice."

But this utopian vision has not come to pass. Consider one of the banes of Indian existence: alcohol. As early as 1786, Bernardo de Gálvez's *Instructions* had included liquor among the items Indians should be given free as a means of weakening them. In 1850, Mexicans plotted the Ramos massacre by inviting Apache to a long drinking bout that left them helpless. American traders regularly plied Indians with whiskey or rum

In 1887, a year after the last Apache surrendered to the U.S. government, youngsters gather outside a public school built on Arizona's San Carlos Reservation.

in order to fleece them of valuable goods. Indeed alcohol became so potent a weapon that in 1802 the U.S. Congress passed the Trade and Intercourse Act. Its main provision authorized President Thomas Jefferson (1801–09) to regulate and even prohibit the sale of spirits to Indians, not as punishment but as a means of protection against swindlers.

Yet alcoholism continued to plague American Indians throughout the 19th century and well into the 20th. In recent years, the government has tried to discourage alcohol abuse among Indians—as well as among other groups—but with negligible success. Statistics released in 1983 by the U.S. Department of Health and Human Services showed that the percentage of alcohol-related

deaths among American Indians was nearly five times the figure for other ethnic groups. And a report issued in 1985 by the Indian Health Service concluded that death from alcoholism among Indians between the ages of 25 and 34 occurred 11.2 times more frequently than for all other Americans of the same age. Among those between the ages of 35 and 44, the rate is 7.7 percent higher; among those between the ages of 45 and 54, the rate is 4.8 percent higher.

The various 20th-century Apache bands have struggled valiantly to overcome hardship against odds no less imposing than those they faced in earlier times. Consider the case of the Western Apache. In the early 1900s, many of the 1,811 Western Apache estimated to live

Reservation life was filled with hardship and deprivation. In this 1880 photograph, impoverished Apache line up for weekly rations on the San Carlos Reservation.

APACHE RESERVATIONS: 1890

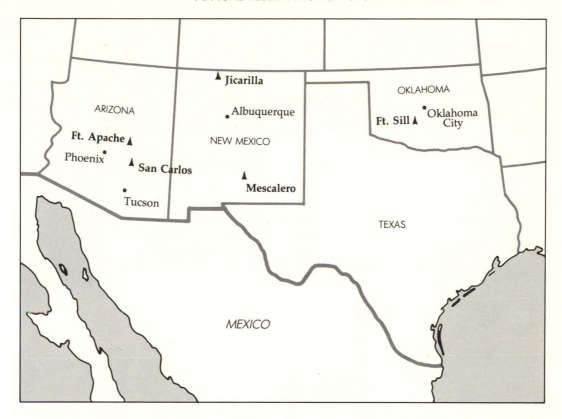

on the Ft. Apache Reservation gave up their effort to live off the land and began to work for wages. In 1907, the U.S. Army employed 80 men to cut hay for horses—rather as Lieutenant Whitman had done 36 years before. Dozens more worked as cowboys. In 1918, the Apache were encouraged to begin cattle ranching, and by 1931 they owned more than 20,000 head. In the 1980s, cattle raising remained a major industry on the San Carlos and Ft. Apache reservations. Another industry, lumber, attracted the Apache in the 1920s and has become a major source of income, employing 200 men and processing 50 million feet of board per year. In the 1950s, a third type of business—outdoor recreation—emerged as a mainstay of Apache employment, as the people drew on time-honored skills to develop camping areas and build cabins.

This income enabled the people to bolster their food supply. They bought flour, coffee, sugar, and beans and added these goods to their traditional diet. Many Apache, however, continue to live in dire poverty on the Ft. Apache Reservation. A study conducted in 1969 indicated that 49 percent of the Apache living on the reservation earned less

In the 20th century, both alcoholism and racial prejudice continue to haunt American Indians, as the sign posted in this Montana bar demonstrates.

than $1,000 annually, including welfare payments—vastly below the national average. Eighty percent of Apache homes fell below normal standards—90 percent lacked heat, 74 percent lacked indoor plumbing, and 46 percent had no electricity. The average house had only two rooms.

The Mescalero have not fared much better. In 1881 General John Pope declared: "It is idle to talk of civilizing the Mescalero Apache. They are savages, pure and simple, and in the country they occupy, with the inducements to raid and the present management of the tribe, it is worse than childish to believe that they are being, or ever will be, reclaimed." Three years later a priest from Lincoln County, New Mexico, tried to introduce the band to Christianity and baptized 173 people. The next year the government established a Court of Indian Offenses, run by the Mescalero themselves, who held judicial hearings, passed verdicts, and issued sentences.

Still, the Mescalero sought to preserve their customary life. They settled in isolated groups and observed their traditional habits as much as possible. At the end of the 19th century, the government redoubled its efforts to "civilize" the band. American officials supervised a reservation on a wagon road along the Tularosa Canyon, near present-day Mescalero, New Mexico,

off Interstate Highway 70. Eventually, the Mescalero began to settle in town, and other Apache joined them. By 1915, leaders of the local groups were meeting with BIA officials, and in 1936 the Mescalero proclaimed a tribal constitution under the terms of the Indian Reorganization Act (IRA), passed by Congress in 1934. This bill empowered the newly created tribal governments to negotiate with federal, state, and local authorities. The IRA attempted to weaken the vast power of the BIA and

In the mid-20th century, Mescalero Apache tried cattle ranching on their reservation in New Mexico's Tularosa Canyon. Profits were marginal.

to restore some autonomy to Indians. As was the case with the Western Apache, Indian agents assumed that agriculture would provide the economic base for reservation life. But water was scarce in the Tularosa Canyon. Enough existed to irrigate only 300 acres. Agents next promoted raising sheep and goats. But the land lacked vegetation for grazing. Cattle ranching suited the terrain better, but the income it produced could not support the Mescalero. They added to it marginally by cutting timber.

Reservation life proved so unrewarding that in 1946 the annual income for one-third of reservation Indians averaged less than $500, while the other two-thirds lived on less than $1,000. In recent times, the Mescalero have turned

to tourism and recreation as a means of improving their standard of living. They have developed a resort hotel—the Inn of the Mountain Gods—golf courses, an industrial park, and other enterprises in New Mexico.

The band's population has increased slightly. In 1988 the Mescalero numbered about 1,700. Unemployment remains a problem. As much as 70 percent of the work force may be without jobs at a given time. Education is one solution. In 1972, 19 Mescalero were attending college, and the number has increased since then.

Destitution also marked the early reservation days of the Jicarilla. Again, the area they were given—the Jicarilla reservation in northern New Mexico—proved unsuitable for agriculture. Also,

Jicarilla schoolboys play basketball outside a dormitory in Dulce, New Mexico, on the northern border of their reservation.

Hardship still marks life on the San Carlos Reservation. These four men were unemployed in 1973, shortly after a survey found 923 of the reservation's 1,122 homes unfit for habitation.

the climate and limited acreage made cattle raising difficult until the government enlarged the reservation in 1907. Timber harvesting did not provide a realistic alternative because of legal complications and confusion about policy. Disease and malnutrition took their toll. From 1905 to 1920 the band's population declined from 995 to 588. In 1917, the Indian agent reported that 90 percent of the school-aged population suffered from tuberculosis.

The government finally acted in 1920, and within a decade health improved on the reservation as tuberculosis was brought under control. Sheep raising proved a viable industry—as an individual rather than collective enterprise. Some Jicarilla turned a profit and the standard of living rose. Like the Mescalero, the Jicarilla organized a tribal government in 1937 under the terms of the IRA. They also established a tribal corporation to direct the reservation's economy. Income from livestock rose, along with health standards and the size of the population.

Sheepherding remained the mainstay of the band through the 1940s; the reservation's natural resources pro-

The symbol of Apache strength is the century plant. It lies dormant for 15 years, then suddenly blossoms, scattering seeds on the desert ground.

vided a substantial income. Gas, oil, and timber reserves were all abundant. The Jicarilla managed to turn these resources to their advantage and phased out sheepherding. No reason remained for living off the land, and they moved in increasing numbers to Dulce, the agency headquarters. By 1954, 80 percent of the Jicarilla lived within 7 miles of the agency.

Like other groups, the Jicarilla tried to assert more control over their own affairs and formed a governmental council. The BIA, however, still regulated their lives. The council usually rubber-stamped federal programs and carried them out with Apache funds.

Although the Apache have struggled valiantly to adjust to the American way of life, its underlying philosophy continues to seem alien to them. Americans showed no understanding of, among other things, the southwestern landscape. The Apache revered everything that grew on the desert—the century plant, for example. This unique plant stores nourishment for 15 years, then thrusts a 6-foot stalk into the air, from which pollen is scattered. The stalk then topples and the plant dies—

a cruel fate, but one expressive of the region. The Apache understood that nature did not overflow with generosity. Mere survival required enormous effort.

The Apache traditionally accepted life on the terms offered by nature. They felt no need to tame it, to batter it into submission, to despoil its deserts and deplete its resources. They were born of the land, and they lived by its rules. But the newcomers thought otherwise. The Spaniards viewed the land materially, as property and as the instruments for their private projects and dreams of power and wealth. Estevanico escaped servitude and tricked himself out in finery. Coronado dreamed of glorious conquest and riches. The Americans were equally stricken with avarice. Many lusted for gold, silver, and other ore deposits that could be gouged out of the soil. This craving lured them to the southwest, where they thoughtlessly killed buffalo, which for some of the Apache had been

a source of food, clothing, and tools. Similarly, the Americans had no qualms about driving the Apache off their ancestral homelands and destroying their communities. As Frank Lockwood wrote in *Pioneer Days in Arizona*, "Every [white] man had in his heart a burning desire to kill an Apache wherever he could find him."

The arid deserts and forested mountains of the American Southwest were once filled with the Apache. They fought to hold onto their bounty even as they were overrun by white people of various nationalities, who coveted their land and reduced them to a subject people. They struggled to retain their traditional way of life—their customs, ceremonies, folklore, and beliefs.

Today the Apache are trapped between the past and the present. Yet the Apache heritage testifies eloquently to their strength. Like the century plant, this heritage will inevitably blossom and cast its seeds into the soil. Many of them will take root and grow. ▲

BIBLIOGRAPHY

Ball, Eve. *In the Days of Victorio*. Tucson: University of Arizona Press, 1970.

Barrett, S. M., ed. *Geronimo's Story of His Life*. New York: Irvington, 1983.

Betzinez, Jason, and W. S. Nye. *I Fought with Geronimo*. New York: Bonanza Books, 1959.

Buskirk, Winfred. *The Western Apache*. Norman: University of Oklahoma Press, 1986.

Goodwin, Grenville. *The Social Organization of the Western Apache*. Chicago: University of Chicago Press, 1942.

Griffith, A. Kinney. *The First Hundred Years of Nino Cochise: The Untold Story of an Apache Indian Chief*, as told by Ciye "Nino" Cochise to A. Kinney Griffith. New York: Abelard-Schuman, 1971.

Lockwood, Frank. *Pioneer Days in Arizona*. New York: Macmillan, 1932.

————. *The Apache Indians*. New York: N.p., 1938.

Melody, Michael E. *The Apaches: A Critical Bibliography*. Bloomington: Indiana University Press, 1977.

Opler, Morris Edward. *An Apache Life-way: The Economic, Social, and Religious Institutions of the Chiricahua Indians*. Chicago: University of Chicago Press, 1941.

Terrell, John. *Apache Chronicle*. New York: World Publishing Co., 1972.

Waters, Frank. *Masked Gods*. New York: Ballantine Books, 1950.

THE APACHE AT A GLANCE

TRIBE *Apache*

CULTURE AREA *Southwest*

GEOGRAPHY *primarily Arizona and New Mexico*

LINGUISTIC FAMILY *Athapaskan*

CURRENT POPULATION *more than 15,000*

FIRST CONTACT *Cabeza de Vaca, Spanish, 1534*

FEDERAL STATUS *The Apache live on four major reservations. Two are located in New Mexico and the others in Arizona. Each reservation has a tribal government established under the Indian Reorganization Act of 1934.*

GLOSSARY

Apachean Tribal Groups The divisions of the Apache Indians that include the Jicarilla, Lipan, Kiowa-Apache, Chiricahua, Mescalero, and Western Apache.

Apache Nomadic, Athapaskan-speaking Native American peoples of the American Southwest and Mexico.

Athapaskan Among Native Americans, the most widely dispersed linguistic family. Athapaskan speakers such as the Apache can be found not only in the Southwest but also along the Northwest coast, Alaska, and Canada.

Aztec A race of Native Americans that established an empire in Mexico.

Band The smallest, simplest type of politically independent society that occupies a specific territory.

Breechcloth A strip of cloth worn around the hips and groin.

Bureau of Indian Affairs (BIA) A U.S. government agency established in 1824 and assigned to the Department of the Interior in 1849. Originally intended to manage trade and other relations with Indians and especially to supervise tribes on reservations, the BIA is now involved in programs that encourage Indians to manage their own affairs and improve their educational opportunities and general social and economic well-being.

Child of the Water The son of sky god Life Giver and White-painted Woman. He is considered the father of the Apache.

Clan A multigenerational group having a shared identity, organization, and property and based on the belief in descent from a common ancestor. Because clan members consider themselves closely related, marriage within the clan is strictly prohibited.

Gadsden Purchase An 1854 agreement between the United States and Mexico in which Mexico gave up the southern parts of Arizona and New Mexico in return for $10 million.

Gran Apacheria The Spanish term for Apache territory. It included New Mexico and parts of Texas, Colorado, Kansas, Arizona, Oklahoma, and northern Mexico.

Treaty of Guadalupe-Hidalgo The 1848 agreement that ended the war between the United States and Mexico. In exchange for $15 million, Mexico agreed to accept the Rio Grande as the southern border of Texas and to cede the territories of California and New Mexico to the United States.

Killer of Enemies Considered by some Apachean groups to be the primary cultural hero instead of Child of the Water.

Lakota Native Americans who inhabited the plains of Nebraska, North and South Dakota, and Wyoming.

Life Giver Sky god or the god of the sky. In Apache mythology, he was credited with creating the universe.

Masked Dancer Supernatural being called upon in curing ceremonies.

Mescal A type of liquor distilled from maguey plants.

Nanta Apachean term for leader.

N'de, Dinï, Tindé, or Indé The terms, translated as "the people," by which the Apache call themselves.

Pawnee Native Americans of the Caddoan-speaking family. They inhabited the Platte River valley of Nebraska.

Pima A division of Native Americans living in the Salt and Gila river valleys.

Power In Apachean religion, a good and/or evil force that affects human lives.

Presidio A Spanish term for fort.

Pueblo A Spanish term for a town or village of certain southwestern Indians; also the name of the group of Indian peoples of the Southwest who inhabited these villages.

Reservation A tract of land set aside by treaty for the occupation and use of Indians; also called a reserve. Some reservations were for an entire tribe; many others were for unaffiliated Indians.

Santa Fe Trail A trade route between Independence, Missouri, and Santa Fe, New Mexico.

106

Shaman A priest who uses magic for the purpose of curing the sick, divining the hidden, and controlling events.

Sobaipuri A Pima tribe of Native Americans living in the San Pedro and Santa Cruz river valleys.

Tipi A conical dwelling of the Plains tribes. It consists of a framework of circular poles brought together at the top and covered with animal hides.

Treaty A contract negotiated between representatives of the United States and one or more Indian tribes. Treaties dealt with surrender of political independence, peaceful relations, land sales, boundaries, and related matters.

Tribe A type of society consisting of a community or group of communities that occupy a common territory and are related by bonds of kinship, language, and shared traditions.

Ute Part of the Shoshoneon-speaking division of Native Americans who inhabited Colorado and portions of Utah.

White-painted Woman Earth Mother. In Apache mythology, she is considered the mother of the Apache.

Wickiup A brush shelter or mat-covered house used by southwestern Indians.

Witch A user of evil power.

ACKNOWLEDGMENTS

AP/Wide World Photos, pp. 16, 36, 41, 42, 99, 100, 101; The Arizona Historical Society, pp. 15, 22 *left*, 24, 25, 29, 87; The Bettmann Archive, pp. 14, 22 *right*, 23, 26, 27, 32, 40, 44, 46, 48, 58, 59, 62, 64, 65, 68, 69, 72, 74, 76, 77, 79, 80, 83, 84, 88, 90, 91, 98; courtesy of the Denver Art Museum, cover; Michael Melody, pp. 12, 20, 66, 102; Museum of the American Indian, Heye Foundation, pp. 21, 30, 37, 49, 50–51, 52–53, 54–55, 56, 92, 94; Organization of American States, p. 70; Special Collections, University of Arizona Library, pp. 18, 35, 86, 95, 96.

Maps (pp. 2, 60, 97) by Gary Tong.

The author would like to acknowledge the generous assistance of Joe McQuay, Jeff Seibert, Craig Ehrlich, and Hugh Ripley.

MICHAEL E. MELODY received a Ph.D. in political science from Notre Dame University in 1976. He has been on the faculty of both Notre Dame University and Kenyon College and is currently associate professor of social science at Barry University in Miami Shores, Florida. His many publications on the Apache include *The Apaches: A Critical Bibliography* (part of the *Bibliographical Series* of the Newberry Library Center for the History of the American Indian), "Maka's Story" (*Journal of American Folklore*), and "Lokata Myth and Government" (*American Indian Culture and Research Journal*). He is also editor of the *Native American Policy Network Newsletter*.

FRANK W. PORTER III, general editor of INDIANS OF NORTH AMERICA, is director of the Chelsea House Foundation for American Indian Studies. He holds a B.A., M.A., and Ph.D. from the University of Maryland. He has done extensive research concerning the Indians of Maryland and Delaware and is the author of numerous articles on their history, archaeology, geography, and ethnography. He was formerly director of the Maryland Commission on Indian Affairs and American Indian Research and Resource Institute, Gettysburg, Pennsylvania, and he has received grants from the Delaware Humanities Forum, the Maryland Committee for the Humanities, the Ford Foundation, and the National Endowment for the Humanities, among others. Dr. Porter is the author of *The Bureau of Indian Affairs* in the Chelsea House KNOW YOUR GOVERNMENT series.